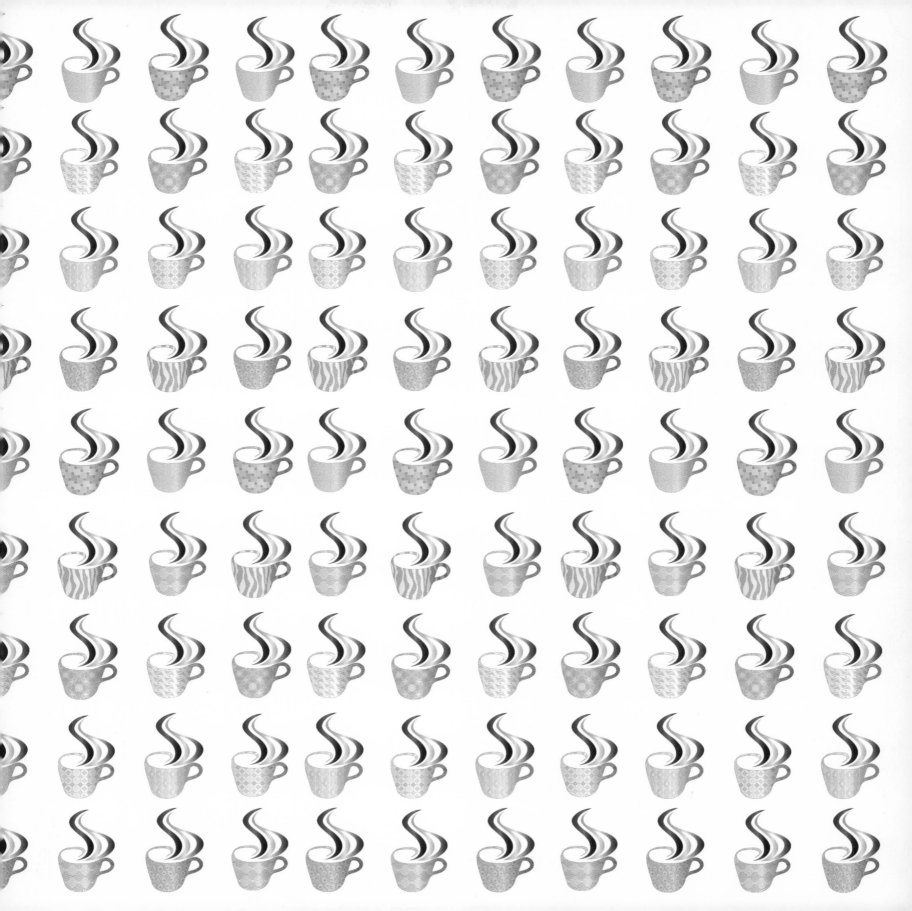

CREATING
A STIR

125 YEARS OF S.D. BELL'S OF BELFAST

WRITTEN BY

BARRY BELL, ROBERT BELL AND KEITH DRURY

WOODSTONE BOOKS

WWW.WOODSTONEBOOKS.COM

ILLUSTRATION AND BOOK DESIGN: KEITHDRURYART.COM

S.D. Bell and Co. 1953

CONTENTS

FOREWORD

The idea for this book arose from a conversation with my nephew, Robert Bell. We both felt that we should mark 125 years of trading not just by producing a historical account of our association with Belfast and with tea and coffee, but also by paying respect to those who in former years guided the company through economic depression, World Wars and local civil unrest. It is perhaps appropriate that I should pen this Foreword as I have spent over 60 years of my life fully employed in the firm. I left school in 1952 and went straight into the business as it was what I had always wanted to do. Even as a toddler, the 'party piece' my father taught me was to wrap up little parcels in paper and snap the string with my fingers!

Tea and coffee are fascinating products, and are perhaps today's most globally important non-alcoholic beverages. Their universal appeal stems from their transition from luxury to necessity in just a couple of centuries, and their role as a source of comfort and stability to aid the human condition. Taken to relax and invigorate, they are pleasant social tools, icebreakers, stimulants to aid conversation, and emollient to comfort the lonely. In Western society, we hear the words, "Let's put the kettle on," not just at times of trouble, sorrow and despair, but also during times of celebration. Tea and coffee oil the wheels of commerce too; in the Istanbul Grand Bazaar, the carpet salesman will entice the tourist with, you've guessed it, a glass of sweet, black tea!

For over 3,000 years tea has been recognised by the Chinese as having medicinal qualities, but it was not accepted in Western society until the 17th century, at which point it was

the greatest luxury. Even in mid 18th century London, the camps were divided between Dr Johnson's "health drink" and Charles Wesley's "Stimulant of the Devil". Coffee, on the other hand, was always recognised as a stimulant and was of course the catalyst for business that fuelled the Lloyd's Coffee House and the fledgling international insurance market. It is now one of the most heavily traded international commodities and, like tea, supports the livelihoods of hundreds of millions of people worldwide. Both beverages are enjoyed in such a great variety of ways, and yet we all seem to hold very personal preferences as to the nature of the brew, be it the particular method, strength, accompaniment and even the time of day.

It is our hope that you will find enjoyment in these pages; you may even learn some new facts about tea and coffee along with the history of our family firm. Perhaps a long-forgotten memory will be triggered. We found the research and writing quite a tough challenge as a huge quantity of used books, invoices and brochures were given up as salvage during the Second World War in order to help the war effort. However, it was not paper that kept this firm trading successfully for 125 years, but the determination of a great many, including John, Sam, Bob, Alastair, Robert and myself to provide our customers with the very best possible blended tea and roasted coffee. That, and of course the loyalty of our customers over the years, of whom, I hope you, dear Reader, are one. If that is so, then thank you for your help along the way!

WBSBell

W.B.S. Bell,
Chairman and Managing Director, 1983–present

DESTINY'S FIELD

John Bell said nothing in reply to the bailiff's words but watched him leave on his pony and trap. The sound of hooves and carriage wheels were still clearly audible on the dry ground of Major Cooper's field but John Bell was oblivious to its mocking ring. Tucking his loose shirt into his breeches and throwing aside the old weathered jacket and the long sleeved waistcoat he was wearing, he took to the fields with the run of a man who had looked destiny in the face and knows he only has a few minutes to run it down, before his life and the life of his family are altered forever.

The rough grass lanes which meandered lazily by the sides of fields may have never encountered such a charge; a galloping man who cleared the ruts and sheughs with a sure footedness that would have evaded John had it been any other day. John understood that destiny is not necessarily the first thing that is offered to us but rather the ultimate course that remains after all other courses have been run through. John's destiny was not going to be delivered by a bailiff riding a pony and trap. Instead, it would be decided where all things were decided, in Stewartstown, County Tyrone at the Great Hall before Major Cooper. This imposing building was clearly visible only a mile away from the field in which John laboured.

As John ran, his mind recalled some of the other farmers he had grown up alongside in Stewartstown. Like him, they knew the land and the crops they grew. They had been taught by their fathers who had in turn been taught by theirs. Unlike today, John and his peers lived in a small world where the boundaries of their existence did not run far beyond their farms and rarely further than the nearest town. But their times were changing. Landlords of tenanted farms were beginning to move from arable farming to livestock and so bailiffs were becoming a common pestilence, removing small farmers from all they knew and the land they relied on. All of a sudden they could be cast out into a world they neither knew nor wished to know. John Bell had heard the stories and said goodbye to many old friends. For those who neither had the strength nor fight to outrun the bailiff's carriage, they joined the line awaiting the vessels at Belfast which ferried them to new lives in America. Once gone, no one heard from them again. There was no way of telling whether their lives were good or otherwise. John did however know that when an Irishman leaves Ireland, a little part of him remains behind, and he is no longer the man he once was.

And so John ran, tearing over hedgerows, clearing loose stone walls and leaving new paths where he made his course over the hills that led up to the Great Hall. When he arrived, the bailiff's pony and trap were just beginning to come into sight at the end of the gravel lane leading to the manor. Appearing on the grounds of the manor like a man who has been fettered and driven in a wild chase, Major Cooper immediately noticed him and calling him by name exclaimed,

"My goodness, John Bell! What's the matter?"

"Major, are you going to turn me off my land?"

"Indeed I am not, I never heard of such a thing," the Major replied with some incredulity.

"Well Major, I have your word and that's good enough for me."

John Bell turned and looked at the bailiff who had now pulled up alongside them and whose face looked as though he had seen two John Bell's, in two places at the same time. As before, John said nothing to him, but this time he parted at a walk and returned to the fields where he had been working.

This is a story of a man who outran destiny, the story retold by his son, Samuel David Bell to Sam's grandson, William Smyly. The story was of course important to him, for had it not been for that adrenalin-soaked charge through Cooper's fields all those years earlier, a ship would have ferried them away to a distant land and there would not have been any Irish-raised Samuel Bell, nor the Coffee and Tea emporium he established in 1887. This Coffee and Tea House still trades in speciality coffees and teas at 'Bell's corner', where East Belfast's Upper Newtownards Road runs

John Bell outside his tenanted homestead along with two of his daughters, Co. Tyrone.

to meet the busy traffic passing through the intersection of the Knock Road and Parkway carriageways.

It is with pleasure that we welcome you to this book which seeks to recount the story of S.D. Bell's Coffee and Tea House which now celebrates 125 years in business. Throughout the course of this book we hope to introduce you to some of the stories of the company during its years of business in Belfast. It is our hope that through this book you will appreciate the passion that has driven the Bell family in its relentless endeavour to provide the most exquisite beverages from coffee beans and tea leaves, roasted and blended on site, only yards away from the emporium. That relentless passion in pursuit of a singular goal is drawn from the personality of those family members who have been roasting and blending as master craftsmen of their trade through 125 years. It is the same passion that drove the father of S.D. Bell through the fields until he reached Major Cooper's manor house ensuring that his family remained in Ireland and, although unknown to him, he thereby created the circumstances that destiny required to establish one of Belfast's oldest companies and a brand synonymous with fine Irish coffee and tea.

Samuel's love of horses stemmed
from his early home life.
Pictured here is his Father W.J. Bell
on the Stewartstown farm

THE BIRTH OF A COFFEE AND TEA LEGEND

Samuel David Bell was born in 1868, the fifth of nine children of John and Sara Jane Bell. He was raised in a staunch Presbyterian family, a family who believed in hard work and noted any absence of the same. While we may not have the full story of his childhood, we do know that by nineteen years of age he had travelled to Belfast, leaving behind the poor economic conditions of rural life to embrace the poverty and hardship of life in the city. When Samuel arrived in Belfast he was without any financial resources and so he took a job as a shop assistant at Dunwoody and Blakely, a general provision store, at Ann Street in Belfast. His intention in due course was to submit himself to training in Theology with a view to entering the Ministry of the Presbyterian Church. To facilitate his studies he took lodgings at 41 Fitzwilliam Street next to the University, a house which had only been built in 1885 on a street just beginning to take shape.

However, as a happy coincidence, Samuel met a girl by the name of Jeannie McCausland with whom he fell in love and later married. Fortunately her father owned a linen mill and was therefore a man of some means. Without doubt, this made it possible for S.D. Bell to put his entrepreneurial talents to good use in developing his own firm.

One of these enterprising schemes involved an unusual arrangement with Dunwoody and Blakely. In return for an investment in the firm, S.D. Bell expected to be freed from other commitments so he could devote himself to studies for the Church. By deriving an income from the firm, he would

Samuel David Bell

13

An old letter penned by S.D. Bell. It was written later in his life after he had moved to reside at Princeton House, Bangor

be in a position to support himself through training for the ministry. However plans, even good plans, are vulnerable at best and it soon became apparent that Dunwoody and Blakely was at risk. The two older partners wished to retire and problems developed as they tried to pass the management of the company on to younger hands. When S.D. Bell was informed of the problem it was suggested that he must re-join the business. No matter how he might approach the situation, his studies for the Church would need to end. If he remained at his studies the company would fail, and if he turned his full attention to the business, the company might stave off bankruptcy but this would be at the cost of leaving his studies and investing all his time in the grocery and hardware business. Given that either way the outcome would be the end of his studies, Samuel chose the only viable option and entered fully into the business of grocery and hardware retail.

However, he did have one requirement: if he was to return and allow the older partners to retire the new management would have to go so that he could take over the running of the store in its entirety. On the settling of these new terms, S.D. Bell became the owner of a small grocery and general store establishment. We must assume that the means allowing him to do so came from his new father-in-law, Matthew McCausland. This begs the question whether those same means could not have kept him at college and in his studies, for Matthew McCausland was also a fellow churchman. This would seem to indicate that Samuel Bell had two broad passions: the first was to succeed in the business of retail service and the second was to succeed in the business of heavenly service. Samuel wisely chose the former as with this choice both ends could be achieved. It is possible to be a successful businessman who pursues all things heavenly but it is difficult to be a clergyman who pursues all things worldly! So by 1887 Samuel had paid his former partners at Dunwoody and Blakeley for their share of the business and he began to trade, with no surprise, under his own name. By 1890 Samuel's new firm is recorded in the Belfast and Ulster Directory under the entry 'Bell, Samuel David and Co., Tea Merchants and Family Grocers, 54 Ann Street, Belfast.'

Samuel David Bell

TRADING CONDITIONS IN BELFAST c1887

When we celebrate the birth of S.D. Bell's Tea and Coffee House in 1887, we need to remember that business in those days was far removed from what we are accustomed to today. S.D. Bell's did not begin as a Tea and Coffee emporium. The economic conditions in Belfast in the late nineteenth century would not have supported such a singular venture. That said, Belfast was not what we might immediately imagine either. Belfast was a rapidly developing city of commerce built on the twin economic pillars of shipbuilding and linen. Later, this strength would also prove to become its weakness. As long as shipbuilding and linen were in vogue as tradable global commodities, Belfast would enjoy prosperity, but on their decline, the city's fortunes would ebb as the tide went out to lift the boats of other industrial prospectors and nations.

When S.D. Bell established his firm, Belfast was not yet a city but was formally defined as a 'town' or 'borough'. However, one year later in 1888, Belfast was granted the status of 'city' by Queen Victoria. Samuel set up shop at a time when Belfast Corporation was still building their network of sewers and when horse-drawn trams ran through the city streets. At this time he would have neither heard of Belfast City Hall, the Albert Bridge or the R.M.S. Titanic. Instead, in the same year as he established his business, the 1887 Crimes Act was passed. This law allowed trial without jury to try to confront rising land offences committed by tenant farmers who were experiencing difficulty in paying rents that had been fixed in more prosperous times. At the same time, government, trying to take control of an ever-worsening situation, followed a course of appeasement and concession to both sides and other laws such as the Land Acts of 1881 and 1887 were introduced. The intention was to try to ensure fairness in land rents and to curb practices of tenant evictions. All the same, the period was a time of turmoil and culminated in what has become known as the time of the 'Land War'.

At this time the White Linen Hall still stood on the grounds of the now present City Hall but it was a time of prosperity and massive change. By the end of the nineteenth century and the beginning of the twentieth, Belfast had become one of the great industrial cities of the known world, something we forget too easily. It was for this very reason that Belfast City Hall was built marking the town's new elevation to a city and celebrating the wealth and fortune of its prosperity.

Vanity Fair caricature of Charles Boycott
1881

FARMING CONDITIONS

On many Irish estates landlords granted reductions or other concessions. Pressure was sometimes brought to bear on landlords by ostracising those who would not co-operate. In 1880, Captain Boycott, who was a land agent in County Mayo for an absentee landlord, gave a new word to the English language. Boycott refused to lower his rents, his tenants were ejected, and his family became a target of retaliation as farm workers would not harvest crops and local tradesmen withdrew their services. Captain Boycott returned to England but the practice of 'boycotting' remained.

The population of the city of Belfast grew from about 174,000 in 1870 to almost 387,000 by 1911, representing 122% growth. In the 1870s and 1880s the city's housing stock quadrupled as streets of terraced 'kitchen-and-parlour' houses were built to accommodate the workers from the mills, factories, and shipyards of the new vibrant industrial city. In 1870 the shipyard of Harland and Wolff constructed a floating dry-dock and launched five vessels with a total tonnage of 15,571. Housing in Belfast improved over the period but Belfast had its fair share of slums and associated health problems. These were the days of Samuel Bell. Exciting days of change and growth and building – a kind of pre-incarnate Celtic Tiger but one built on hard work and tangible products rather than on the speculative manoeuvres of the recent past.

However, whilst this was an ideal time to establish a business, fine coffee and tea were still the drinks of the wealthy and were not enjoyed by the ordinary man on the street who did not have the means for such luxurious purchases. For this reason S.D. Bell's began as a general merchant's

Upper Newtownards Road, circa 1905

store trading in staple commodities and so coffee roasting and tea blending was not conducted in those early years.

By 1890 S.D. Bell decided to expand his operations to the leafy, suburban Upper Newtownards Road and built three houses at the present Knock site. The first imposing house, Wandsworth Villa, sat on the corner of the carriageway where the Northern Bank is currently located. The shop was situated on the ground floor of this house and accommodation for Jeannie and himself, and their young family was located above the premises. Beside this building, just beyond the far end of its yard and stabling area, S.D. Bell also erected two further semi-detached houses further down the Upper Newtownards Road. These two houses still stand on their sites adjoining the Leaf and Berry Coffee and Tea House. Samuel placed these two homes into the names of his wife and her sister. Thankfully his father-in-law only had two daughters, and no sons, so the building of further homes at this stage was unnecessary! However the acquisition of the land and building of the homes served a dual purpose. The new Knock site had more room than that available

at Ann Street so there was more room to stable and graze horses, an animal Samuel was very fond of. The larger premises also provided the room the company needed to expand its operations. (Jeannie's long-time maid Nisa joined the household, and insisted on the family cow joining them so that Wandsworth Villa could incorporate its own dairy!) The other benefit the building project created was to provide work for the builder, well-known to S.D. Bell, as he was none other than Samuel's brother, Wilson Bell.

1929 Armstrong Siddeley
Four wheel brakes, adjustable seat, swivelling headlamp and rattle-proof side screeens.
£250

Horses were of course not his only choice of transport. In later life, Samuel developed a penchant for luxury cars. Business records include mention of Armstrong Siddeleys and Lanchesters, amongst others.

"Coffee in England always tastes like a chemistry experiment."

Agatha Christie

KNOCK AT THE TIME OF S.D. BELL

The term 'middle class' is an epithet of recent invention. For a long time life was simple, you either lived in the manor, or you served the manor. The notion that you might live well doing neither seemed ridiculous. S.D. Bell was however one of those new inventions, a social experiment exploring the middle floors of the building of societal hierarchy.

Following the tragic occasion of the potato famine, many tenanted farmers had neither the ability to feed themselves nor had they the resources to pay rent to their landowners. So many poor people began what must have seemed a frightening pilgrimage to the cities in pursuit of work to ensure survival for themselves and their families. This paved the way for the dramatic population growth that Belfast experienced from the 1850s onwards. However, it created another problem. At that time no one had envisaged towns growing in such a fashion. The rich and landed gentlemen and their families lived in the cities which made for excellent places to enjoy and indulge their social lifestyles. These people lived in their fine homes in places like Donegall Square now situated in Belfast's city centre. People flooded into the small town of Belfast living in crowded accommodation where diseases spread like wildfire. With the transport system of horse trams arriving in Belfast in 1872 and the industrialisation of the town with shipyards, ropeworks, brickworks, linen mills, dairies and bakeries, it was clear that town centres were no longer places for well-to-do families to live and so many moved away from the city and built large estates and houses on the hills around Belfast. Fine houses were created on the Antrim Road, in Malone, Belmont, Fort William and Knock. Wandsworth Villa was one such house.

The earliest houses built in the Knock area were constructed in the 1860's, the first being Beaconsfield House, where the Marie Curie Hospice is located. Brooklyn House was also built on the site where the PSNI headquarters is now located.

At that time Knock was not a residential area, and the original deeds confirm only green fields of Ballycloughan between Knock and the Belmont Road. Yet there is a significance as to why S.D. Bell built Wandsworth Villa where he did. Across the road from the house (where there is currently a newly constructed Doctor's surgery) was the tram depot. Until 1905 the tram was simply horse-drawn and owned by the Belfast Tramway Company, but in 1905 the route was electrified and transferred from private to public ownership and was run by the Belfast Corporation. An electric tramway then ran from Belfast ending at Wandsworth Villa. Prior to 1895 no trams could run as far as Knock because Connswater Bridge was too

White Linen Hall demolished in 1890s to make way for Belfast City Hall.

THE HISTORY OF BELFAST TOWN
IN THREE PARAGRAPHS

The old Belfast Town was established in the early 1600s by an English landlord, Sir Arthur Chichester, whose descendant would be the Marquis of Donegall after whom many of the streets of modern day Belfast are named. Their home in the original Belfast Castle (nothing remains) was near High Street and the name is still retained in Castle Street and Castle Lane. The present Belfast Castle at Cavehill was built later in the 1870s.

The old Belfast Town was centred around a sandbank and river crossing close to Queen's Bridge and the mouth of the Farset River. In fact, the name 'Belfast' derives from an old Gaelic reference to a sandbank. The original walled town where people lived took in the area roughly encompassing Donegall Street, Royal Avenue, Chichester Street and High Street. As the town grew, Belfast extended and the first shop in Donegall Place was established in the 1850s. At that time wealthy merchants lived in houses around this area but the site of all those houses is now occupied by shops or office blocks.

Old street directories indicate that centre of town residents included well placed individuals such as doctors, merchants, clergy and other professionals and business people. By early the early 1820s the area around College Square was developed with large Georgian terraces, as was Wellington Place, Linenhall Street, Howard Street, Great Victoria Street and Bedford Street. Some good examples of these houses can still be seen in Donegall Pass.

narrow for trams to pass. The bridge was subsequently widened and this allowed traffic and the people who benefitted from it to move further away from the centre of Belfast. At this time there were three small bungalows on Wandsworth Road and these served as billets for the men operating the horse-drawn trams. As the trams were largely used during weekdays for commuting into Belfast, their route was extended at weekends in order to avail of their spare capacity and they ran as far as Dundonald so that people could visit the cemetery located there.

Further to the horse-drawn trams and the later addition of electric trams, the Belfast and County Down railway opened a station at Knock on the Sandown Road in 1850 and this main line ran until 1950 when it was closed.

Given that from 1905 a modern, reliable and 'fast' transport system of its day was in place, the area surrounding Knock became much more accessible. Shortly afterwards, more middle class housing sprang up and paved the way for what would become a popular residential area.

However, whilst the area was beginning to develop, no shops existed at this time on the Knock or Upper Newtownards Roads. This was mainly due to the fact that Viscount Bangor, Sir Thomas McClure, Marquis of Downshire, sold parcels of land with leases which prohibited the use of premises built for commercial use. The leases instead required the construction of large residential houses and gardens.

By the 1870s a number of houses had been built in gated communities; perhaps fifteen to twenty large houses would be neatly built as a road with gates at each end, examples of such included Knockdene and Cherryvalley.

As the area began to develop, benefitting especially from the new transport systems and a burgeoning economy, a new middle class emerged and began to move into the area. These new

Wandsworth Villa, Upper Newtownards Road, circa 1905, looking towards Belfast. The two houses behind S.D. Bell's still stand today

colonisers of the outskirts of Belfast came not only with their families and money but also with a fair degree of pretention and aspirations of upward social mobility. Given their new position as middle class home owners, their homes enjoyed names which reflected their occupants' new found status. They therefore named their streets after desirable English locations such as Grosvenor, Sandown, Hawthornden, Windsor, Cliftonville and Balmoral; all aspirational addresses taken from the great estates of Britain.

SAMUEL DAVID BELL – THE PERSONALITY

By the time Samuel Bell arrived in Belfast he already was well acquainted with the work of a grocer as he had served an apprenticeship with a Mr Robert Woods, a grocer in Stewartstown, County Tyrone. He had also gained further experience in Portadown and Armagh before coming to Dunwoody and Blakely in Belfast. However, his interests extended far beyond the confines of retail and General Provisions. Throughout his life he maintained a deep faith and took a great interest in religious, philanthropic and missionary work. He contributed to the work of a number of churches and served as an elder in the Presbyterian Church for sixty years. He was a founder and trustee of the Shankill Road mission and the first chairman of the Qua Iboe mission for Africa established by local Nigerian Ibuno chiefs in response to concerns they held regarding the increasingly destructive superstitious practices followed by their own people. These involved slavery, human sacrifice and the strangulation of twins on birth. S.D. Bell was able to put his gifts as an administrator to good use to assist the mission which was established in 1887. He also employed these same gifts as Vice President of the Committee of the Portstewart Convention.

Samuel David Bell

However, his sights were not only focused on faraway lands but were also keenly focused at home and on his own city. He was a member of the Belfast Civic Union and Belfast Citizens Association and was associated with the Irish Temperance league by serving on its committee.

Beyond his philanthropic interests, Samuel also pursued interests allied to his core business as a grocer and tea merchant, becoming chairman of the Board of Management of the Belfast and North of Ireland Grocers' Association. He was also distinguished by being made a Fellow of the Grocers' Institute in London which is an honour reserved for very few in the trade. For the years 1921–1922 he filled the position of President of the Belfast and District Chamber of Trade and gave it a very progressive lead from the chair. His insistent advocacy of various reforms,

Jeannie Bell

particularly in the line of public economy, affected not only traders' interests but benefitted the welfare of citizens generally. In recognition of the public service he had offered to the city he was appointed to the Commission of the Peace in 1923 for the City of Belfast at the age of 55.

From even such a brief analysis, it is clear that Samuel Bell was an able man who devoted himself wholeheartedly to any task he chose to undertake and perhaps the success he achieved in life can in some manner be attributed to how his philanthropic virtues ran in tandem with an administrative deftness. History often records as great those who combine their abilities with a real desire to help others and invariably these are the people who change the world and leave behind a legacy for others to follow. S.D. Bell was such a person, honing his commercial abilities

Postcard used as a receipt, acknowledging £25 received from S.D. Bell, 1898. The expenditure was in connection with S.D. Bell's building at Knock and the receipt is signed by his brother.

through the course of his apprenticeships gained in various places. His passion, however, for ordinary people came from the things he witnessed when he spent many hours in the slum districts of Belfast working alongside church missions. These areas were cramped and dangerous and parts of the waterfront have been variously described as desperate with crime and inhumanity. The experiences S.D. Bell had in these places shaped him into the man he became and are now a part of the rich and valuable heritage of S.D. Bell's coffee and tea.

However, even great men must also be afforded some relaxation in life. For S.D. Bell, 'light entertainment' related to the horse and as far as he was concerned the finer the horse the better. In fact, William Smyly, a grandson of S.D. Bell once wrote of him, *"If horses had had a more respectable place in his kind of Presbyterian society he would have given his life to them in preference to tea."* However, in S.D. Bell's world, horses were transport engines and not steeds ridden side saddle over grass meadows to the neighbouring Manor House for afternoon tea, even though he may have been the provider of the commodity in the first place! Samuel never ceased to regret horses' poor reputation as animals bred simply to pound the old cobblestone streets of Belfast. The typical example of a horse in Belfast in those days was

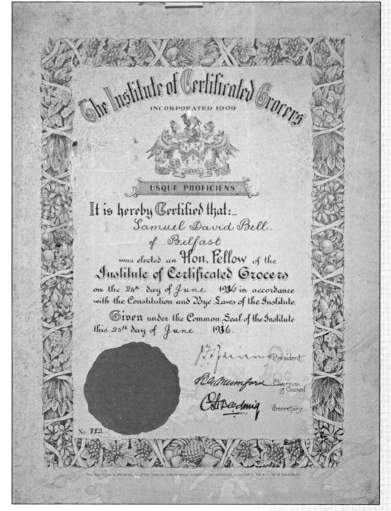

S.D. Bell's Fellowship of the Institute of Certified Grocers

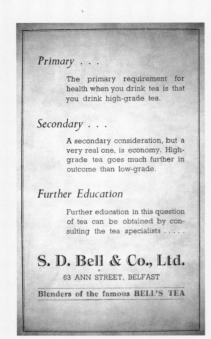

An old newspaper advert extolling the virtues of good tea.

IT PAYS TO BUY GOOD TEA

S.D. Bell bought tea at the London tea auctions. Traditionally Bells would outbid most of the major English tea houses and they frequently paid the top prices in London sales. This practice gained the company a reputation for high quality teas regardless of price. The end product then depended upon the skills of the master tea blender to create a blend of tea which bettered the main brand rivals for quality and price. One of S.D. Bell's early skills was to pay attention to the quality of tap water, including water hardness, in differing market areas to ensure that the final blend of tea was appropriate for the water used in those regions. The higher prices associated with S.D. Bell's quality teas, was reflected in their early advertising strap line, 'Good Tea Goes Farther.'

Today the London auctions do not figure so prominently. The world is a smaller place and most importers shop directly from the plantations or in the auction houses of the producing country.

the huge mule bred from a Clydesdale mare which was destined to pull coal wagons and loaded drays around the docks. However, S.D. Bell maintained that a fine blood horse put down its feet more gently on the cobblestones and lasted longer on the hard stone paving. Whatever excuse he gave, the end was the same, S.D. Bell's tea and produce was ferried on some of the finest and shapeliest legs ever seen in Belfast at the time.

One happy coincidence of his love of fine horses was that it may even have contributed to his marriage to Jeannie who would become his lifelong companion and wife. The story is told how she was scolded by her sister for her insistent peeping out through the windows in the front room whenever he rode past on a large and fine horse. Many years later she admitted to it claiming, *"He wore a brown suit and rode a big horse and he looked lovely."* Another version of the story is a little more kindly to Jeannie because apparently S.D. Bell took the route past her house for no other reason than to be seen by her and, given that he wrote her love letters and at least one poem, it would appear that he was as culpable in the matter as she.

Life had now become a very different place for Samuel Bell compared to the days when he had envisaged entering the life of the Church to serve as a clergyman. Since his exit from Queen's University Belfast, his life had followed a very different trajectory from what it would have otherwise had it not been for the failure of Dunwoody and Blakely necessitating his return to the world of general provision. Somewhat ironically however, his acquaintance with Queen's University was not going to end with his studies of Greek, Hebrew, chapter and verse. In due course he returned to Queen's, this time not as a student but rather as an honorary lecturer on food and particularly tea. He also lectured for twelve years on tea to the grocery classes of the Department of Agriculture and spoke to students at the Municipal Technical Institute.

Finally S.D. Bell passed away aged 88 on Sunday 3 July 1949 at Princeton House, the home he had built and lived at for some 30 years on Princetown Road, Bangor, County Down. He was buried, like so many of the City Fathers, in the City Cemetery.

S.R. Bell's licence to retail Methylated Spirits 1937

Mr S.R. Bell

SECOND GENERATION BELL

S.R. BELL

Following Sam's death, his son Samuel Robert (S.R. Bell) came to be the lead figure at the company. He was known by close family and friends as "Rob" but in order to avoid confusion given the preponderance of Bells in the firm, he was called "Mr Robert" or "The Guv'nor!" and in commercial circles he was known as "Bob". He had joined the firm following the Great War, having received his decommissioning papers in 1919. Thus he followed in his father's footsteps in the manner of what was common to leading businessmen of that period. He would mount his motorcycle (with sidecar) to drive round the highways and byways selling tea to his retailer customers. Business grew as the entire community gradually became addicted to what was once the preserve of the wealthy, and by 1924 S.D. Bell's had become a Limited Company.

The retail business had expanded in Ann Street, necessitating a move in the late 1920s from No. 53 to a larger corner site at 63 Ann Street, incorporating an adjacent four-storey building at 83–85 Victoria Street. S.D. Bell's quickly became synonymous with the best tea, coffee and delicatessen goods available. A period of steady growth followed until the shock of the Second World War stopped the firm in its tracks.

Bob is credited with the introduction of mechanisation of the roasting process at S.D. Bell's. Coffee roasting involved a metal cylindrical

2nd. Lieut. S.R. Bell

KEEP YOUR POWDER DRY – AND DISTANT

The virtues of S.D. Bell's tea tasting abilities found new acclaim following a complaint registered by a customer who said Mr Bell's reputedly high quality tea was not to her liking at all. She returned the packet and showed it to Mr Bell himself. After some minutes of careful examination and smelling the aroma with all the skills of a master, he was able to satisfactorily address the problem. "Madam, you have kept your tea along with your soap powder!"

This was impressive, but the lady and those standing by were even more impressed when he continued by naming the very brand of the powder which had led to the whole sorry incident. Advice was offered to the lady that a tea caddy would solve all her problems and return her to the famed flavour and aroma of S.D. Bell's tea.

S.D. BELL & Co.
TEA IMPORTERS
GROCERS
—AND—
COFFEE DEALERS

Head Office,
53, ANN STREET.
Wholesale Stores,
63, CHURCH LANE.

Branch Store,
KNOCK.

THE GREAT BELFAST FLOUR WAR

As a boy, one of the tasks allotted to S.D. Bell had been to mill the flour. Over time he came to understand what an important foodstuff flour was to the poorer family. This recognition of flour as a basic necessity may have been the reason for Samuel breaking a cartel of grocers in later life, as recorded in the minutes of the Board of Management of the Belfast and Northern Ireland Grocers' Association of 8 Oct 1920. At a time of severe shortage of flour, the cartel pushed up the price from 4s /4d to 5s /2d per stone. These high prices began to hurt the poorer household. The unscheduled arrival of a ship laden with flour into Belfast gave Sam the opportunity to show that he was a man of the people. He purchased the entire ship's cargo and started selling flour at the former price.

It was not long before the prevailing price fell back to its original 4s / 4d.

Illustration of Ann St.
premises 1956

drum which was turned by hand. The beans were roasted when they fell and passed through the flame. However, the manual design of the roaster meant that the success of the roast depended on the constant revolutions of an individual's rotating elbow. A slow turn or pause might cause the beans to be unevenly roasted. This scenario prompted Bob to look for a solution and one immediately suggested itself. He had just purchased a car and so his motorbike, and specifically the engine, was not required at the time. So with a few adjustments to the sprockets and gearing and the addition of a belt or two, the old manual roaster was soon transformed into a modern automated machine which turned at a regulated speed. Unfortunately S.D. Bell's archivist has not been able to find any photographs of the improved machine or indeed Health and Safety certification!

If Bob was a fan of the motorbike, his dear wife, Annie Scott Blue, daughter of the renowned preacher Alexander Wylie Blue, was certainly not! She may or may not have approved of mechanised

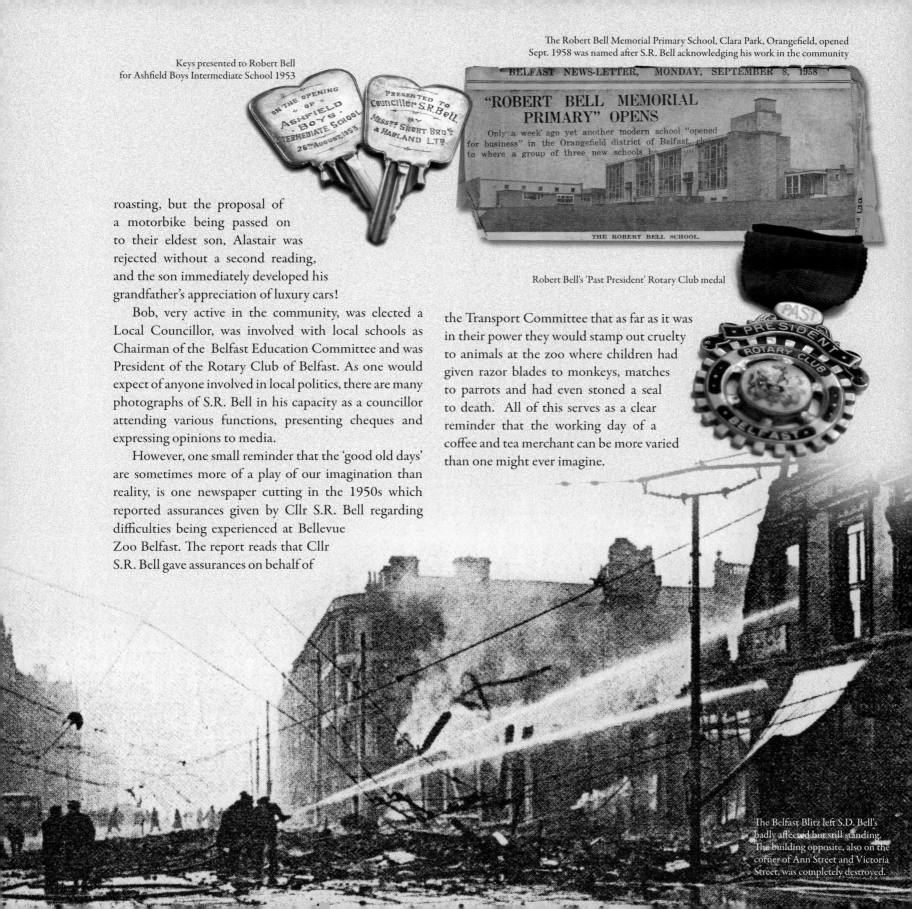

Keys presented to Robert Bell
for Ashfield Boys Intermediate School 1953

The Robert Bell Memorial Primary School, Clara Park, Orangefield, opened
Sept. 1958 was named after S.R. Bell acknowledging his work in the community

BELFAST NEWS-LETTER, MONDAY, SEPTEMBER 8, 1958

"ROBERT BELL MEMORIAL PRIMARY" OPENS

Only a week ago yet another modern school "opened for business" in the Orangefield district of Belfast, close to where a group of three new schools ha...

THE ROBERT BELL SCHOOL.

Robert Bell's 'Past President' Rotary Club medal

roasting, but the proposal of a motorbike being passed on to their eldest son, Alastair was rejected without a second reading, and the son immediately developed his grandfather's appreciation of luxury cars!

Bob, very active in the community, was elected a Local Councillor, was involved with local schools as Chairman of the Belfast Education Committee and was President of the Rotary Club of Belfast. As one would expect of anyone involved in local politics, there are many photographs of S.R. Bell in his capacity as a councillor attending various functions, presenting cheques and expressing opinions to media.

However, one small reminder that the 'good old days' are sometimes more of a play of our imagination than reality, is one newspaper cutting in the 1950s which reported assurances given by Cllr S.R. Bell regarding difficulties being experienced at Bellevue Zoo Belfast. The report reads that Cllr S.R. Bell gave assurances on behalf of

the Transport Committee that as far as it was in their power they would stamp out cruelty to animals at the zoo where children had given razor blades to monkeys, matches to parrots and had even stoned a seal to death. All of this serves as a clear reminder that the working day of a coffee and tea merchant can be more varied than one might ever imagine.

The Belfast Blitz left S.D. Bell's badly affected but still standing. The building opposite, also on the corner of Ann Street and Victoria Street, was completely destroyed.

THE DAY THE WAR BROKE OUT

The Second World War had a huge impact on work at S.D. Bell's. Products like (non-essential) coffee and even 'essential' tea, which had been beginning to develop in the marketplace became subject to rationing. Customers had to register with their chosen grocer; shops were then allocated food, tea and coffee and other wares according to the number of customers they had on their books and the size of their families. As such the government became the main buyer of commodities, and these procurements were fairly distributed amongst grocers and other shop keepers. This had a dramatic affect on businesses whose market position depended on their ability to source fine products or to provide high quality produce. The coffee which was bought and supplied by the government was a poor quality African Robusta bean. During war years, ships were vulnerable to attack and carrying high quality beans at high prices was therefore an unnecessary risk when there were more important things to be concerned about.

As the skills of being expert buyers of tea and coffee during war years (rationing continued until 1956) were somewhat redundant, Bob bought a 40 acre farm in Ballywalter in 1938 and evacuated his family there. He only worked about two or three days in the business because the work of the business now focused on the management of the simple resources they were provided with from central government. At the time the company had an excellent manager, so there was no real need for Bob to always keep a watchful eye on day to day matters. He became what might be called a 'gentleman farmer', taking the bus up to Belfast on the days he needed to travel to the business.

However, in war times everyone finds themselves making their own war effort and one night each week Bob took his turn on 'fire-watch.' This involved going onto the roof of May Street Presbyterian Church, located just at the rear of Belfast City Hall. He shared his watch with his father-in-law the Reverend Alexander Wylie Blue, who was minister of the church at the time. In 1941 they spent two terrible nights smothering incendiary devices with sand, or casting them into waste ground in the street where they would create less damage. Bob described how relieved he felt to return to the Ann Street premises finding it unharmed, although the building across the road was totally gutted. He was greatly upset to hear that one of his young female employees perished in the bombing.

Ration books for petrol used by S.D. Bell's

ABSTRACT OF THE ACTS IN FORM PRESCRIBED BY THE MINISTRY OF LABOUR AND NATIONAL INSURANCE

To be kept posted in factories at the principal entrances or in such parts as an Inspector may direct.

FACTORIES ACTS
(Northern Ireland), 1938 and 1949

NOTICES ETC. SHOULD BE SENT TO:
Chief Inspector of Factories.

Appointed Factory Doctor *Dr Kirk*

Name of Occupier *S D Bell & Co Ltd* *127 Ann Rd*

Address of Works *83 Ann St* *Belfast*

Belfast

THIRD GENERATION BELLS

ALASTAIR AND BARRY BELL

S.D. Bell and his son S.R. Bell made a formidable team as they worked together in partnership. During this time, Marian Hogg, Bob's sister, had also been appointed to the Board, remaining a Director until her death in 1968. In time the next strong relationship team was of two brothers, following S.R. Bell's death at 62 in 1956. These two brothers were David Alastair Wylie Bell and William Barry Scott Bell, respectively eldest and third sons of S.R. Bell.

Before we focus on these siblings bound together in business, let's glance at another two of Bob's children. The Bell Family had, until this generation, not excelled in musical spheres. His youngest child, Hilary Anne, a pupil and Head Girl at Ashleigh House School in Belfast, was a talented pianist, and followed a career as Company Pianist with the major ballet companies in England. She spent 14 years with Sadlers Wells Royal Ballet rehearsing and performing extensively in the United Kingdom and many other countries. She remains a non-executive Director of the business.

History has a way of fulfilling its own destinies. It may have been extremely gratifying to S.D. Bell, albeit from beyond the grave, to see his grandson, Robin McCausland Bell take up the cloth, and serve as a Presbyterian Minister for 43 years, in Raphoe and Ballindrait in County Donegal, and First Kilraughts in County Antrim.

Lady Astor:"If I were your wife,
I would put poison in your
coffee."

Winston Churchill in reply:
"If I were your husband,
I would drink it."

ABSTRACT

WELFARE.

DRINKING WATER.—An adequate supply of wholesome drinking water, with an upward jet convenient for drinking or suitable drinking vessels with facilities for rinsing them, must be provided. If the water is not a public main it must be approved in writing by

47. TWO SHIFT SYSTEM.—The Ministry may on the application of the occupier authorise the employment of women and young persons over 16 on a shift system subject to such conditions as the Ministry may consider necessary for their welfare and interest. The shifts must not average more than eight hours per day or end later than 10 p.m. on Saturday) it is to be varied with certain exceptions.

BUY INDIAN TEA

EMB

Old sales poster (S.D. Bell's Collection)

CEREALS, CANNED MEATS ETC.

Asparagus Tips, ½ Kilo, Tins
Bamboo Shoots (C) 20 oz. tins
Beans Sprouts (C) 20 oz. tins
Bombay Ducks, Indian, tins
Curry Powder, Madras, tins 16 oz. 8 oz. & 4 oz.   8/4, 4/7
Escargots (with shells) (F) 7½ oz. tins
Frankfurter Sausages (B) 6 oz. tins
Frankfurters in Brine (G) 10 oz. tins
Goulash Beef (G) 7 oz. tins
Goulash Pork (G) 7 oz. tins
Goulash Veal (G) 7 oz. tins
Ham, Bellantini Raw (I) 6½ oz. tins
Herring, Au Gendarme (F) 4½ oz. tins
Macaroni A.P. 16 oz. packets
Lychees (Strawberries) (C) 20 oz. tins
Macaroni, Egg Dwarf, 8 oz. packets
Mangoes sliced Indian, 12 oz. tins
Mushrooms (F) 8 oz. tins
Mussels (D) 14 oz. tins
Noodles, Egg Assorted, packets
Patna Curry Rice, Indian 16 oz. packets
Polenta, Brena (I) 2 lb., packets
Puppodoms, Indian, tins
Ravioli (I) 7½ oz. tins
Ravioli (I) 13½ oz. tins
Ravioli (I) Buitoni 8½ oz. tins
Ravioli (I) Buitoni 20 oz. tins
Sauerkraut (G) Wine 20½ oz. tins
Sauerkraut Dutch 16 oz. tins
Spaghetti A.P. 16 oz. packets
Spaghetti Di Nola 16 oz. packets
Spaghetti with Sauce al'Italienne 10½ oz. tin
Sugo, Sargans (S) 7½ oz. tins
Vermicelli, A.P. 16 oz. packets
Vermicelli, Di Nola 16 oz. packets

SAVOURIES CONSERVES ETC.

Anchovies, fillets of, (P) 2 oz. tins
Anchovies, with capers and pimientos (F)
Anchovies, rolled (F) 3-ring bottles 2
Anchovy Paste (G) 2½ oz. stone Jars
Anchovy Paste (G) 1 oz. tubes
Antipasto (P) hors d'ouvres 4½ oz. ti
Antipasto (F) 3 oz. glasses
Caviare (G) 1¾ oz. Jars
Cranberry Sauce 16 oz. Jars
Creme de Marrons, 2¾ oz. tubes
Delicacies, Assorted, Seven glasse
Gaffelbiter, 1½ oz. tins
Guava Jelly 16 oz. Jars
Lax, in oil (Smoked Salmon) 1¾ o
Olives, Black (I) 6 oz. Jars
Pate de Foie (S) 3½ oz. tins
Pate de Foie (B) 3½ oz. Jars
Pate de Foie Terrines 1½ oz.
Pate de Foie Terrines 1¼ oz.
Patum Pepperium, 2½ oz. Jars
Peeled Shrimps (N) 3¾ oz. ti
Pickles, Mixed (C) 14 oz. J
Pork & Goose Liver Pate (F
Saffron, thimbles
Sweet Cherry Jam 16 oz. J.
Swiss Cherry Jam 16 oz. Jars

SAVOURIES CONSERVES ETC., CONT/D.

S.D. BELL & CO., LTD.
IMPORTED & SPECIALITY FOODS.
November, 1955.

Tabasco Puree (C) 14 oz. Jars
Tart Cherry Jam 16 oz. Jars
Tomato Paste (I) 16 oz. tins
Tomato Paste (I) 7 oz. tubes
Tomato Paste (I) 2¼ oz. tins
Tomato Puree (I) 5½ oz. tins
Torrone (I) Almond Candy, blocks
Truffles (F) 30 grm. tins

COCKTAIL BISCUITS ETC.

Assorted Cocktail (H & P) 9 oz. tins
Cheeselets   packets
Celery Sticks (PF) packets
Cocktail Assorted (Romary) packets
Cocktail Assorted (Romary) packets
Football Biscuits (PF) 8¾ oz. packets
Parmesticks (Cheese) tins
Reception Canapes (H & P) 6 oz. drums
Roka Cheese Crispies, (H & P) 7½ oz.
Salzletten Wafers (H & P) packets
Savouries Cocktail (Romary) packets
Twiglets (Dutch) Tins
Savouries Cocktail Savouries, 1 oz. packets
(Cheese, Celery & Sherry) (Surrey) 5 oz.
(PF) packets

BISCUITS ETC.

Honeycake, Dutch per cake
Macaroons, (I) 8 oz. packets
Petit Fours 8 oz. boxes
Pumpernickel (F) 8 oz. packets
Volkornbrot (G) packets

B = Belgian
F = French
N = Norwegian

C = Chinese
G = Chinese
P = Portuguese

D = Danish
I = Italian
S = Swedish

FOR COCKTAILS.

Cocktail Cherries Bottles
Midget   2¼ oz.
Baby   4 oz.   1/6
Small   7 oz.   2/3
Med.   ¼ litre   3/3
                         5/-

Salted Jordan Almonds
2½ oz. Btls.   3/-
4 oz. Tins   2/6

Salted Nuts.
Tins Cashew 1 lb.   7/6
Tins Cashew ½ lb.   3/6
Tins Peanuts 1 lb.   3/6
Tins Peanuts ½ lb.   2/6
Tins Mixd. 1 lb.   7/6
Tins Mixd. ½ lb.   3/6

Cocktail Onions.
5 oz. (White, Yellow,
green & Red)
4 oz. Btls.   2/6

Cocktail Gherkins

Sherry Olives.
4 oz. Btls.   2/2

Manzanilla Olives with
Pimiento
12 oz. Btls.   2/10
6 oz. Btls.
2½ oz. Btls.   5/-
                  2/10
Cherry Sticks etc.   1/9

*
*
*
*   *

Price lists from 1955 show a mouth-watering list of exotic produce. Many of these goods, if they had ever been seen in Belfast, had certainly not been obtainable since before the Second World War when rationing was so prevalent.

This Aladdin's cave of grocery which S.D. Bell's became offered everything from a well hung smoked side of bacon to Beluga Caviar or, dare I say it, smoked German cheese!

But history repeats itself too. Just as S.D. Bell had to cancel his studies, Alastair Bell interrupted his studies in Agriculture at Queen's University when S.R. Bell became ill in 1950. He commenced work with the company, still at 63 Ann Street at £4.00 per week. Barry, his junior by some five years, left school after Senior Certificate and immediately joined the company in 1952 at £3.00 per week.

Barry's earliest business memories include cattle being driven through the street to the market at the top end of Oxford Street, and Ned, the scrap collector's penchant for "vegbitle sloop". Gangs of shipyard workers would stream twice daily over the bridge, a sea of cloth caps. Some, more than a few, developed a taste for loose, pitted "Hallowee" Dates, to be purchased at – guess where – for less than 8d per lb! Coffee was being roasted daily in Ann Street, and the aroma in the surrounding city squares, avenues, entries and lanes is still recalled by many Belfast citizens.

There followed a period of business growth, massive changes in commercial practices, economic shocks, political turmoil, terrorism and radical changes in shopping habits. As had gone before, the brothers

Mr Alastair Bell

BON VOYAGE

The post-war years were certainly a time of commercial growth. Barry Bell, (of whom, much more anon), recounts a time in the late fifties and early sixties when S.D. Bell's had contracts with the Admiralty to provision warships from Britain, Spain and France, when they frequently called into Belfast Port to top up their supplies.

These ships ranged from submarines to destroyers to frigates but the occasion of this story centres on the Canadian aircraft carrier HMCS Bonaventure paying a return visit to Belfast. She had been built by Harland & Wolff in 1943 with the name HMS Powerful, and may also have undergone a refit at this time.

The usual format was for Bell's to supply the ordered goods as speedily as possible and then in their own time forward the account to the Admiralty in quadruple. This time, however, things went rather differently. Having been on the quayside at 6.30am supervising the arrival of lorry loads of milk, vegetables, Bramley apples, along with multitudinous other items, including of course, coffee and tea, 24-year old Barry was sitting in the office relaxing, peacefully content in the knowledge of a huge task successfully

completed when a telephone message came through. He was informed that the carrier was leaving on the tide in two hours and was urgently requested to come down with the bill for payment as "this ship pays its own way!"

Frantically the account was written up and Barry took a taxi to the dockside knowing that he had no time to park and walk. Most of the gang planks were away, and as he found his way on board past a huge refrigerated store where hundreds of sides of meat were hanging, deep down through the vast ship to the Purser's office, he could feel the mighty rumble of the awakening engines. The Purser opened a safe the size of a garden shed and started handing out bundles of notes!

After a quick handshake and a "good luck" by both parties, Barry retraced his labyrinthine steps to the about-to-be-lifted gangplank, and arrived ashore, hearing a cheery cry from a Jack Tar, "There's nice girls in Canada you know!" At once, Barry found himself on the quayside, alone and vulnerable, with armfuls of notes and the prospect of a long walk back to HQ!

made a good working partnership. Alastair focused on expanding the 'wholesale' side of the business, developing retailer relationships, and marketing high grade Tea and Coffee into quality shops, delicatessens, hotels and restaurants. This growth was somewhat restricted by the development of multiple super-and hypermarkets who were less inclined to offer terms acceptable to the small business. Still, also through a number of dedicated sales representatives who regularly traversed the province, dozens of new accounts were opened up, many of which continue to buy S.D. Bell's tea and coffee today. Alastair also contributed greatly to the wider commercial life of the city, as Chair of the Belfast Chamber of Trade, serving on the Distributive Industries Training Board and Grocers' Association. He married Jane Barklie Price in 1961, and they had three children, Catherine, Robert and Alison.

Barry was based at the Company Headquarters in Ann Street, as well as at Knock, and also took responsibility for a small shop in Botanic Avenue which traded well between 1961 and 1982 when civil unrest made this impossible. The Botanic Avenue shop is fondly remembered by former Queen's University students.

Mr Barry Bell

Seamus Anthony Close joined S.D. Bell's in 1970, having graduated with a Diploma in Business Studies. He took over the position of Company Secretary after the retirement of Mr Ernest Rea JP, who had filled the post since 1956. Ernest was the much loved Uncle of Alastair and Barry and he had been greatly respected in his time as Chairman of the Belfast Water Board, and for his Boys' Brigade connections.

From the first, a firm friendship grew up between the brothers and Seamus. Barry valued Seamus's cooperation particularly after Alastair's untimely death in 1983.

Seamus' interest in politics took him firstly onto Lisburn Borough Council, serving from 1973 until 2011, when he retired as Alderman, and was awarded the Freedom of the City of Lisburn. He also served as an MLA at Stormont from 1982–1986, and again from 1988 until 2007, and for his services he was awarded an OBE. As Mayor of Lisburn in 1993-4 he raised £105,000 to aid the Malcolm Sargent Children's Cancer Unit.

Seamus Close, Company Secretary 1970–present

Ernest Rea, front row second from right. Pictured with members of the Water Board

HOW 'PERUVIAN HEIGHTS' GOT ITS NAME.

Alastair often let his dry sense of humour intrude in the naming of products and enjoyed telling this story:

"As post-war rationing gave way to a reasonable supply of quality coffees, we received a sample of Peruvian Arabica which we adored, yet we were informed that as the London coffee broker fraternity did not rate it highly, none was earmarked for the UK Market. So the only way we could source it was to purchase direct, 200 sacks, each of 140lbs, and ship it direct from Lima. The coffee was duly loaded onto a passenger liner as deck cargo, but the liner ran aground off Bermuda. In order to lighten the load, the coffee had to be thrown off into the shallows.

Eventually the coffee was retrieved, and although the insurers were prepared to indemnify us, the salvage company offered to try to dry it out and ship onward, an offer we accepted. Having cleared customs (after some extensive deliberation, something to do with the coffee having been further processed), the shipment finally arrived in Belfast. We couldn't wait to get it into the roaster, and found that immersion in the Atlantic Ocean had if anything improved the coffee further. Tongue firmly in cheek, the coffee which had lain in the 'depths' was christened 'Peruvian Heights.'"

To this day, S.D. Bell's has never been out of stock of fine Peruvian Arabica, although it does not always benefit from saline immersion!

Gone... that aroma of coffee in Ann Street

1973

Belfast Telegraph, Tuesday, June 19, 1973

THAT certain something in the air that ed to announce you ere in Ann Street in elfast has gone.

That familiar aroma freshly roasting coffee as, if you'll excuse the xpression, ground to a alt.

For the old-established rm of S. D. Bell closed wn their shop at the rner of Ann Street at e week-end, and a amiliar sight—and smell the city centre—has one.

Samuel David Bell erved his apprenticeship the grocery trade in tewartstown, Co. yrone, and worked in ortadown and Armagh efore coming to Belfast.

He was manager of unwoody and Blakely 53 Ann Street and hen the owners retired e bought the business nd founded the firm of . D. Bell in 1888.

His son, **Samuel Robert** expanded the tea istribution side of the usiness and they ought larger premises Ann Street, where the irm has remained ever ince.

The business further expanded to the Upper Newtownards Road in 1934 and a warehouse was added there later, and to Botanic Avenue n 1961.

TROUBLES

Sadly, 'The Troubles' had a significant impact on the business. The Ann Street premises were extremely exposed to the effect of bombs, bomb threats and consequent security measures, to the point that in 1973, the sad decision was made to leave the City Centre, and relocate all operations to suburban Knock.

'No Entry' sign outside Ann Street premises
Belfast Telegraph 'An ULster Log', 19 June 1973

35

Artwork depicting the Ann Street premises which have now been demolished.

When Barry was interviewed by the Belfast Telegraph in June 1973 he said, "Although we will be in business at the other two shops, it is not without feeling that we are leaving Ann Street. We had a security gate right outside the shop and we felt that now was the time to close and re-organise."

The Troubles fostered a stoic attitude as one had to 'get on with life' as best as possible, frequently defying the ever real threat to life and limb which was often closer than one realised.

No successful company stands still, and the Bell Family showed grit and determination perhaps inherited from the great John Bell himself, in confronting an adverse environment, and recreating the business at Knock. As proud providers of tea and coffee, it was an obvious, and ultimately ingenious move to demonstrate the products, for consumption on the premises. The first tentative steps to build a coffee and tea house were taken and it would eventually become a local icon.

Alastair's death in 1983 was, of course, a great personal shock to the family, and had a massive impact on the business, coming at a time when wholesale sales into other retailers were under massive pressure from large producers, and increasing commercial demands from ever-larger and more powerful customers. The 'dry' teas and coffees which defined the business for over 100 years, had to be maintained at all cost. These were the 'Crown Jewels', the S.D. Bell's 'DNA', whose packaging continues to be graced by the image of Samuel David Bell. But for the survival of the firm, cash, and cash flow were the life blood. Barry dug deep.

LIFE IN THE TRENCHES

Protecting this life-blood supply was not easy. In 1974, the forecourt of the Knock premises was vested by the Department of Environment to facilitate the widening of

A CLOSE SHAVE

At the height of 'The Troubles' the custom was for most city centre workers to head for home early in case streets were barricaded and bus services withdrawn. Having had to stay longer than normal on one particular day, Seamus was making his way to his car, which was parked on a nearby site.

A voice without any apparent source in the vicinity of a dark doorway 'politely' told him to avoid walking across open ground as there was an unfriendly sniper in an alleyway near his car.

Such was Seamus' stubborn attitude, he continued undeterred by his 'traditional route', got in his car and drove away. Only later did he realise the degree of danger that he had been exposed to.

On another occasion, a vigilant police officer had noticed a hearse, with coffin, parked in a nearby street. Not aware of any funeral activities that day, he called a bomb alert, and the area was quickly evacuated. As Barry and Seamus were exiting themselves from the business, the blast came, and with it, a coffin handle clattered onto the pavement in front of them.

One Friday, when there were bombs exploding at regular intervals throughout the day, one of the largest explosions went off at Oxford Street Bus Station, about one third of a mile from S.D. Bell's shop. A screwdriver embedded itself in a coffee tin, a few feet from where Barry was standing.

the Upper Newtownards Road. This was sizeable area to lose, and Alastair had set in motion a claim for loss of a potentially valuable site.

The actual work did not commence until 1985, and S.D. Bell's had to resort to a tribunal for compensation, which was not settled until 1988.

Barry and Seamus worked together to minimise the appalling effect that the road works had upon business, as the shop had been surrounded by digging machinery and service trenches. At this time, Barry had no hesitation in inviting Alastair's widow, Jane, and his colleague and friend Seamus, to strengthen the Board of Directors.

Barry and Seamus worked for several years on the policy of "if you don't need it, don't buy it", in order to keep the Company solvent after the difficulties of the past decade. But standing still was not an option; in 1986, Bell's was back in the City Centre again, taking a unit in the new Hi-Park complex.

So, summoning the determination of his great grandfather, Barry proceeded to vault metaphorical hedges and fences, stretching every sinew to grow and maintain the coffee and tea sales through retail and wholesale channels, while consolidating the cash-generating engine of the Tea and Coffee House that would sustain the small business through economic hardship and civil unrest.

Images displaying the major disruption caused by the road widening scheme, which at the time jeopardised the very existence of the firm. A generation later the ample car parking created continues to be enjoyed by many patrons of S.D. Bell's

LEAF AND BERRY

Whilst the origins of S.D. Bell's once lay in general provision, the firm has changed over the years, as one might expect, and today it specialises in the roasting and sale of fine coffees and teas. Attached to this roasting and blending operation and situated only yards away from it on the Upper Newtownards Road is the "Leaf and Berry" Coffee and Tea House.

Until 1978, the retail business at Knock was primarily concerned with sales to the general public of 'dry' goods, but while large supermarkets and out-of-town shopping centres grew their market share, it was clear that the firm needed to adapt, and how better than to show off the products of which they were so proud? In 1974 the decision was taken to create a small coffee bar area and until 1976 S.D. Bell's ran the parallel business models of coffee bar catering and general grocery provision. In that year the firm decided that the future lay in this new direction and general groceries ultimately ceased to be part of S.D. Bell's product line by 1978. Initially in 1974 the space in the premises

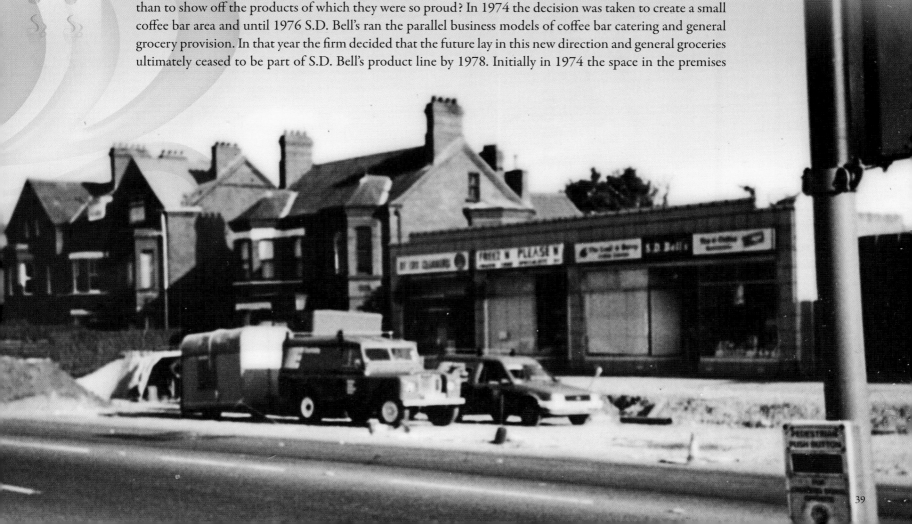

allocated to seating was sufficient for about 20 people, a rudimentary kitchen and servery was created, and 'The Leaf & Berry' was born. At once, it was recognised as a place for local people to meet, socialise and sample the very best tea and coffee. It quickly captured an extremely broad and loyal customer base of business people, young families, courting couples from local schools, tea aficionados and those who wistfully remembered the aroma of roasting coffee in Ann Street, Belfast.

Clearly the availability of parking, the location at the junction of one of Belfast's busiest arterial routes, proximity to local businesses, Civil Service, Parliament Buildings, schools and residential areas, improved its chances of success. The Leaf and Berry underwent several refurbishments until 1987, and had a complete makeover in 1999–2000, by which time seating capacity was approximately 90 covers.

As tastes have evolved, so has the menu which now includes light, continental and full breakfasts, home-cooked lunches and afternoon teas, and of course the full range of espresso, gourmet coffees and fine teas one would expect from a business which has focused on tea and coffee for over 100 years.

Old Uno Hand Roaster.
S.D. Bell's vintage collection

RATHLIN ISLAND SAVED BY S.D. BELL'S

FLY BELL'S

Torrential rain and persistent gale force winds resulted in the inhabitants of Rathlin Island being cut off for three weeks from re-supply by boat from Ballycastle in 1938. As food supplies diminished the Islanders radioed for help. A pilot named Denys Gillam responded to the government's plea for assistance.

He flew a reconnaissance of the most likely landing field, which was only 250 yards long. While he was in the air S.D. Bell & Co. of Ann Street, Belfast, hurriedly prepared a consignment of flour, oatmeal, butter, tea, sugar, lard, paraffin oil, candles, matches, cigarettes and newspapers, which was delivered by S.D. Bell's van to Aldergrove. This was then loaded into a Westland Wallace K5073 and Denys Gillam took off again.

Local priests on the Island lit a fire to create smoke to help guide the aeroplane to its landing area.

The Belfast Telegraph described the first landing by an aircraft on Rathlin as follows: 'To make the landing the plane had to descend very low and hurdle over the roof of a house. The field selected for landing was the best available but it was small and exceptionally bumpy and definitely hazardous for a medium sized bomber.' The feat was repeated the next day in another Wallace K5074.

Denys Gillam was later awarded the Air Force Cross for his airmanship and bravery in undertaking the relief flights. S.D. Bell's did not miss their opportunity either, as an advert appeared in the newspapers headed 'Rathlin Island – supplied at a moment's notice – we can supply your requirements with the same dispatch and satisfaction.'

Shop interior of Ann Street

Whatever happened to Santa?

It was one week until Christmas and Santa was coming to our school. Everyone was waiting for this moment. Near the end of assembly Dr. Hamilton announced "Here is Santa." But he didn't come through the doors. Dr. Hamilton checked all over the school but he wasn't anywhere to be found. All the kids were disappointed so they had to go back to their classrooms. "Where could he be?" I asked some of my friends. They didn't have a clue. The rest of the day was lousy. I got about four sums wrong so did everyone else. We just kept thinking about where he could have been.

After school I did my homework and got changed quickly and went to a coffee shop called S.D. Bells. Pat served us as usual. I took a Mars bar. As usual Dr. Hamilton was sitting with his son. I heard Dr. Hamilton shouting at a man that was dressed up as Santa. It was the man who was supposed to have come to our school earlier in the day. "Where were you?" shouted Dr. Hamilton. "I have a school full of upset children who wanted badly to see Santa, but you didn't come!"

"I am very sorry, Dr. Hamilton" said the Santa. "I was on my way but I got lost. I saw this coffee shop and thought it would be a good idea to come in and ask for directions. Pat offered me a coffee before I could explain my purpose and it was so good that I forgot all about the school and the children and why I had come here in the first place."

When Dr. Hamilton heard the story, he understood because Bell's is a mysterious coffee shop. Santa agreed to come to the school the next day, but promised not to stop for coffee!

Philip Baillie, Room 25

S.D. Bell's, a few pages ago, were able to triumph in the fact that they saved Rathlin Island. Sadly the children of Strandtown primary were to suffer a very different experience.

The letter printed on the facing page, written by Philip Baillie (now a journalist with agency Reuters) of 'School Room 25' sadly says it all.

He tells the story in his own words, recounting the palpable excitement of the children waiting for Santa to come to their school one Christmas. Unfortunately Santa was a no show and the children had to return to their classrooms. As Philip eloquently expresses it, "The rest of the day was lousy."

Enough said!

Later that day his Mother took him to S.D. Bell's to enjoy a Mars bar, a small consolation admittedly. Nothing could have prepared him for what he was about to witness. There he saw the school principal shouting at a man dressed up as Santa.

It turned out that Santa had got lost on his way to the school and stopped at S.D. Bell's to obtain directions. The aroma of the coffee enticed him so much he thought some fortification of the black stuff would be good. Unfortunately he enjoyed it so much he lost track of time and completely missed his appointment at the school.

Philip, ever the diplomat, recounts how the principal understood Santa's pleadings for he too was an aficionado of S.D. Bell's coffee.

Well, we bet that's what he told Philip!

Ann Street Traders' Association heralds the Daleks, Christmas 1965

S.D. Bell's has always entered into the Christmas spirit. At Christmas time the coffee bar is decorated throughout with a particularly homely Christmas feel. Staff and patrons alike become caught up in the festive spirit.

S.D. Bell's while still on Ann Street was part of the Ann Street Traders Association, who at Christmas time made an effort to host special events on the street which added to the atmosphere of Belfast and sought to bring shoppers onto the street. We have included on these pages a few of the sights and sounds of Christmas at S.D. Bell's over the years.

One outstanding tradition has been for Mr Charles Maginess to play the old harmonium located in the shop. The instrument was built by the Bell Organ and Piano Company of Guelph, Canada, in 1887 - the year S.D. Bell's was founded.

Everyone loves Santa!

FOURTH GENERATION BELL

R.W.J. BELL

Few family businesses can boast three generations of uninterrupted family service. To claim four is without question a rarity, and particularly if by way of direct descendancy, father to son, to son to son as became the case when Alastair's son Robert became fully employed by the company in 2006. Such immediacy has facilitated not only the transference of knowledge and skills in a unique manner but has also served to distil a fondness for the company and brand between each successive generation. Fondness, perhaps, is not quite the right word to use, because the family owners do not just feel a 'fondness' towards the brand but rather an inseparable unity with it.

As Robert explains, *"It's not a question of 'ownership' - I don't view myself as owning the company in any way really. Becoming part of a family business like this is about contributing and adding value. I still see myself at best as a trustee. In the same way as I have done, any family member is welcome, who is willing and able to make a contribution of their talents and time."* It is clear that what he is articulating is that in the same way you don't 'own' a family or a child,

likewise ownership is an inappropriate attitude at S.D. Bell's. In fact quite the opposite, instead of the company belonging to the individual, the family members view themselves as being privileged to belong to the company of S.D. Bell's.

Yet while this is the case, Robert does not feel that his joining the company had any inevitability attached to it. This was no arranged marriage made in secret behind old sacks of coffee!

Alastair's three children did however grow up close to the company – that was inevitable, and they all spent school holidays helping out from time to time. One of Robert's earliest memories at the age of eight is being caught in the lift between the third and fourth floors of the old Ann Street premises. It was one of those vintage styled pieces complete with sliding concertina gates like something off the set of a Humphrey Bogart movie. However, on this occasion the young Robert failed to catch any sense of nostalgia and the whole sorry event was indelibly seared into his memory, as it seemed like an eternity before help arrived. His other memories were, on occasion, being chauffeured around the countryside by the van drivers while they made their daily deliveries. And of course, as any young lad knew in the 1970s, being driven around in a towering Bedford van was like winning the X-factor. School holidays were, of course, always punctuated with working in the firm, opening tea chests, blending and packing tea, and from 17 years of age, delivering the same around the country, albeit not in a Bedford van!

> " I never drink coffee at lunch.
>
> I find it keeps me awake for the afternoon.
>
> Ronald Reagan "

49

However, Robert wasn't destined to start immediately behind the counters on leaving school as though that was all life expected of him. Alastair had often reiterated that he should never feel he must follow in his father's footsteps, as he had done. Instead, Robert completed a degree in Business and German at Leeds University. This was something of a novelty in the family firm, as both Samuel and Alastair had started university degrees but never completed them. Perhaps Robert's love of languages and coffee began at this early stage for his father had arranged some Sixth Form work experience with the German coffee machine manufacturer Melitta-Werke (inventors of the filter paper!) Alastair's death at this time put no pressure on Robert to join the company. Instead he was encouraged to pursue his own route in life. Following his degree, Robert found himself working in Glasgow and Newcastle upon Tyne with the Guardian Royal Exchange before being headhunted to join several London based IT companies, one of which included IBM.

Robert was of course always conscious of the old and loved family business and was very much kept up to date by his mother and uncle when he was at home. However, it didn't occupy his waking thoughts at that time and he settled happily into the life he had made for himself and his young family across the water.

In 1999 Robert was drawn back to Northern Ireland and began working in the telecom sales industry for Apion, and then Phone.com, a mobile telecoms software company, as Belfast was becoming a rising star in the global telecoms software industry. But although based 'at home', his job often demanded that he be in as many as four different countries in any one week. Whilst Robert was experiencing some of the world's diverse trends and cultures, the constellation of stars that constituted his life began to include the small planet that is the firm of S.D. Bell & Co. Perhaps its gravitational force had by 2003 begun to exert its pull on Robert for it was in that year that he became actively involved in the company. Between 2003 and 2006 Robert began assisting Barry with a few customer calls, deliveries, and other 'heavy-lifting', and before long, while still fully employed at Openwave Inc. he was marketing S.D. Bell's coffee and tea products around the country. In 2004, Barry asked him to join the Board.

So, on weekdays Robert was in foreign parts selling multi-million dollar telecom deals and on weekends he might be found selling packets of coffee or tea in Howth or Malahide Farmers' markets. Soon Belfast's St. George's Market became an important outlet for

the business, and he quickly built up a 'markets' business unit, taking S.D. Bell's on the road to Dublin, Enniskillen, Derry and Coleraine and other farmers' markets around the Province. This immediately became a profitable vehicle for marketing the firm, reconnecting customers who had got out of the Bell's habit, and finding new retailers to stock the range of coffees and teas. Whilst drawing no actual income from the business at the time Robert was, like successive generations before, learning the business and proving himself in the process, a worthy fourth generation torch bearer.

In June 2006 Robert gave himself fully to working with S.D. Bell's and officially joined the company. The work he had done in those intervening years had been crucial and the

markets continue to be a significant part of the business strategy today, although as is to be expected in any small business, Robert is involved in all parts of the firm, which include the retail shop and coffee bar, internet sales, wholesale sales and markets.

Robert's arrival facilitated a further redevelopment in 2008, with the movement of the packeted 'dry' product lines into the adjacent shop unit. Thus an emporium was created on the main road frontage, giving these products the exposure they had always deserved. This in turn allowed a further extension of the coffee bar, to include a raised platform of loose seating, and brought the capacity to over 110 seats!

Leaf and Berry tea and coffee house and espresso machine

ROASTER TIME

DAY iN the LiFE oF:

A DAY IN THE LIFE
OF A COFFEE AND TEA MERCHANT

6.10am Alarm, with one or two snoozes. Then up, wake the girls, breakfast with a cup of black tea. Check emails and internet orders. Leave home for S.D. Bell's.

7.40am Crank up the roaster and roast four to five batches of coffee. Some are destined for the airport, some for the shop and others for wholesale orders to be filled that day. Coffee has to be fresh, roasted in small batches to order. (The aroma extends for a mile or more. It's one sure way to get the locals up and out of their beds!)

9am Shop opens.

9.30am Check what deliveries need to be made, arrange couriers for anything urgent. Prepare any special orders, such as those from the internet.

10am Check emails again. Check world trade price movements of coffee. Call London brokers, chat with Barry and decide what to buy before placing orders.

10.30am Post arrives. New Seasons Darjeeling tea samples have arrived from Mumbai. Set out Samuel's antique tasting cups, put the kettle on, sit down with Barry and taste the new teas. Make notes and compare. Request prices for teas we like.

11am Coffee may now be taken – a black Americano!

11.05am Coffee shop is full. Chat to a few regulars, meet a new customer and bump into an old school friend.

12noon Back in the office, more phone calls and administration.

1pm Shop full again for lunches. Soup and a roll in the office followed by a black coffee. Discuss Sunday's staffing plan with William, coffee shop manager.

2pm Make a couple of deliveries around the city, and visit

LETTER FROM LINLEY

Ireland's leading Jazz impresario, performer and broadcaster, Linley Hamilton recalls how he became involved with S.D. Bell's.

I remember receiving a phone call from Robert Bell a few years ago, the proprietor of a coffee emporium on the Newtownards Road that for some reason I had thought was part of a church. I was soon to find out that not only was it a Coffee Shop with a belly-busting fry on offer to sink you into your chair and have you stay a while with a caffeine kick and comfortable repast, it was about to become one of the most significant venues for jazz that Belfast has seen in the last twenty-five years.

Robert had been chatting with a friend about starting a live Jazz gig at Bell's, and the friend suggested he approach enthusiastic English sax player, Dan Forshaw. Dan was all business and

a few retail customers asking their opinion on the new coffee tin sample which has just arrived from Hong Kong.

3.30pm Review tomorrow's schedule and deliveries. Telephone a few wholesale customers from that area and prepare orders.

4pm More roasting.

5pm Load the van in preparation for tomorrow's early runs and cash up the shop. Try to lock up by 6pm.

En route home, collect gymnast-daughter in Comber. Phone Linley Hamilton to finalise arrangements for upcoming Jazz gig on Sunday.

EDITORIAL COMMENT:

Something didn't seem to add up to us so we purposely asked Robert, *"Is that all the coffee and tea you drink in a day? We have friends that could make you look like an amateur – don't disappoint us!"*

After some thought Robert tells us he always starts the day with black tea and finishes it with an exotic 'Jasmine Dragon Pheonix Pearl' white tea. From 6.30am he reckons he drinks about seven cups of coffee and at least four cups of tea. *"That makes eleven cups a day,"* we tell him.

Then we ask, *"Does that include all the tea-tasting and coffee-cupping each day?"*

"No, that's extra!" he replies, but of course any formal tea tasting demands a spittoon!

Our faith is restored.

> "Choose a job you love, and you will never have to WORK a day in your life."
> Confucius

---

was keen to take the responsibility on himself to build his profile, create an image, and draw the punters into the venue as the house band. His marketing techniques were refreshing and up to date and they soon had the place bouncing. But rather than just another venue with the same band every week, Robert Bell had a vision. He believed that there were numerous bands and musicians out there that were 'underplayed' in Belfast; guys who played regularly but anonymously maybe doing the jazz in the corner at the drinks reception, the kind of gigs that did not fully represent their talent. You see Robert was an enthusiast. He had a passion not just for coffee but for music, but although a businessman, it was clear that he did not see the music as a commodity, a product that would boost his take.

Robert has shown utmost respect to all the musicians and nurtured his relationship with them. He has followed them to their high profile festival slots, become a fan of the bands and the players and a vital part of their circle and network. People like Mark McKnight and David Lyttle who are significant players on the UK scene took it upon themselves to have S.D. Bell's on their tour circuit when they brought players into

Ireland and the visiting musicians were treated like royalty. This is a genuine touch from a genuine guy, nothing premeditated, just a personal touch from a man who most of the best musicians in the business consider now to be their friend and whose thoughts and opinions on their music they seek with genuine concern, people like Ronnie Greer, Anthony Toner and of course myself.

I am proud of Robert. I am proud of S.D. Bell's. I'm proud that he has made the Sunday into a regular jazz slot with a turnaround of up to fifteen different bands a year with full houses every week and a commitment to make it continue. The value is on so many levels it is hard to measure the full impact that the venue has had on the scene, but one thing that stands out to me is the number of ensembles that have been formed specifically to play with 'musos' being creative to try something fresh, to change their set, to organise guest players and vocalists to share each other's company and their music. That alone makes S.D. Bell's a jewel in the crown of the live music scene here and I consider myself fortunate to be a part of it and all the goodness that it generates, most of which emanates from the man himself...Robert Bell!

JAVA JIVE

It might seem an unlikely decision to open up the business on a Sunday, and it certainly would never have been proposed by Samuel in his day. However, it is also fair to say that nowadays while many worship on a Sunday, even those that do are pleased to watch their football team in the afternoon, go shopping, or undertake other commercial activities.

The Leaf and Berry has been blessed with a core of customers who arrive with clockwork regularity, daily and weekly, Monday to Saturday. With a view to further expanding the customer base by opening on Sundays, Robert felt that there needed to be a reason to visit, rather than the business simply treating this as 'just another day'. So as a one-time musician with a 'good ear', he did what many of us do, who enjoy our passions vicariously through the achievements of others. He proposed in September 2009 a short Sunday 'Jazz Brunch' period from 11am until 3pm.

BBC's Noel Thompson suggested that he have a word with performer, broadcaster and impressario Linley Hamilton, who, thrilled at the prospect of a jazz venue in East Belfast, was eager to help. At once, Sunday's "Java Jive Jazz Brunch" at S.D. Bell's was born. Advertising purely through word of mouth and social media, and well placed ads in the Jazz press resulted in almost every Sunday being a full house, and a constant stream of Ireland's top Jazz and Blues performers offering their services. Every Sunday, any remaining free booths at Bells are quickly occupied by hungry, music-loving local churchgoers!

Barry also freely admits that to arrive into a warm, welcoming coffee bar, buzzing with conversation and with live music of the highest quality is 'good for the soul'. It certainly beats spending cold Sunday afternoons blending and packing tea in those dark 1980s days!

125 YEARS ON

Today Barry and Robert can often be found together in the store or in their small shared office. Yet this is something of the inescapable charm of S.D. Bell's. Barry and Robert epitomise a company that is 'comfortable in its own skin'. "You know", Robert muses, "a small fire will keep you warm, and a big fire can burn you." He knew that for a fourth generation to happen at all, he needed to demonstrate to himself and to the firm that sustainable profitable revenue growth was achievable. In a small way, just like his great, great grandfather, he too found himself with his own 'fields to cross and hedges to vault'. He has an exciting plan to continue that growth through wholesale exports, new retail lines and more live music and events in the Leaf & Berry.

To survive for this long is a tremendous achievement - few companies last this long, most do not. If the firm had continued untrammelled with the growth of the 1910s or 1930s or 1950s, Bell's might be a huge corporation by now, but the ebb and flow of business doesn't have to be like that. The Bell Family have steered this small ship cautiously past some rocks that did not endanger other ships, and safely past other rocks on which larger ships have foundered.

So S.D. Bell's has weathered the storms of life, troubles and recessions but still retains its soul intact. It is not about corporate suites, receptionists and deep pile carpets. There is an intimacy which strikes any first time visitor, and a strange kind of accessibility or reality which has come to elude many modern companies.

To choose S.D. Bell's tea and coffee is to demonstrate an appreciation of the finest of products, created with love, and rooted in values that can only be inherited, not just invented in an afternoon's marketing workshop. Visiting S.D. Bell's is a little like coming home, a safe place to relax and drink a coffee or tea in the midst of an unsafe and unpredictable world. It is almost as though S.D. Bell's has found the secret to packaging the best of the good old days and all the fond memories they invariably stir within us.

Robert and Barry Bell discuss tea buying prices in the S.D. Bell's office

BEAN TO MACHINE

FIRST ORIGINS

*"God created profoundly fallible creatures on this earth,
and human history is mostly the story of error and accident."*
Michael Ledeen

Discoveries are often the happy coincidence of illumination gained in the pursuit of studying something completely unrelated and our human history of scientific discovery has often been peppered with such fortunate accidents.

This method of discovery also explains the origin of the beverage we know as coffee and whilst we may never be able to ascertain precisely how it was discovered, we challenge anyone to refute the account we are about to give.

And so the story is told that in the Ethiopian highlands, many years ago, a goat herder by the name of Kaldi was tending his flock. Being an attentive man, he noticed that when his goats ate the berries from a certain tree, they became so spirited they did not want to sleep at night. In our research we came across some fantastical reports that the goats even danced but we are inclined to think of this as an embellishment of the worst and most serious kind.

Kaldi decided he should take his mysterious discovery to the local monks, they being not just the 'local sages' but also experts in alchemy. After all, were beer and wine not also discovered in the same way? Upon receipt of the strange cherry the monks discovered upon chewing the seed that an extra stimulus was provided, enabling them to stay awake through evening prayers. Perhaps a few nights later the monks decided that a little sleep during evening prayers wasn't such a bad thing after all and threw the remaining beans into the fire. It may also be that they subjected the beans to further scientific research by roasting them. If so, then without doubt a delicious aroma must have arisen and the obvious next step must then have been to put the kettle on and create a brew... and so the very first cup of coffee was born.

As the word of the monks' new discovery moved east and coffee reached the Arabian peninsula, it began a journey which would eventually spread the reputation of coffee around the globe. Today coffee is grown in a multitude of countries around the world and whether it is Asia or Africa, Central or South America, all can trace their heritage to the trees and goats that once inhabited the Ethiopian plateau.

It was the goat!

While we cannot vouch for everything in this story and a few embellishments of our own may have crept into the writing of these paragraphs, there is most likely some truth to the legend of Kaldi and the story of how coffee was discovered. Certainly others agree for Kaldi is a name often associated with coffee shops, coffee roasting brands and coffee equipment suppliers. Most convincingly the legend appears in the Cold Case television series 'Creatures of the Night' and that pretty much swings the story's truth barometer into the area of fact.

The Arabs were not only the first to cultivate coffee but they were also the first to begin its trade. By the fifteenth century, coffee was being grown in the Yemeni district of Arabia and by the sixteenth century it was known in Persia, Egypt, Syria and Turkey. It is claimed that its rise in popularity was in part due to the fact that alcohol was forbidden by the Koran. As it is human nature to seek out some form of stimulation, coffee became an excellent substitute. Had coffee been discovered in some parts of beer and spirit drinking Ireland, perhaps its fame may never have got much further than the Isle of Man!

Coffee was not only enjoyed in private homes but also in the many public coffee houses known as 'qahveh khaneh' which began to appear in cities across the Near East. These venues provided a strong social atmosphere and their presence quickly flourished as they were frequented for a range of social activities including music, performances, chess and the transfer of knowledge. Because they rapidly became centres where information and learning were exchanged, coffee houses came to be referred to as 'Schools of the Wise.' Of course because Mecca was a location which attracted thousands of pilgrims each year, pilgrims were not only fortified by the religious messages they imbibed but also by the coffee they consumed. The 'Wine of Araby' as it was sometimes called spread from Mecca throughout Muslim and Christian territories alike in its own silent mission to conquer the world.

Pope Clement VIII
Patron Saint of Coffee?

By the 17th Century, coffee had made its way to Europe and was becoming popular across the continent. Those who were opposed to the dark beverage did as they have always done when something new and suspicious arises and called the beverage the 'bitter invention of Satan.' In Venice in 1615, the local clergy condemned it and the controversy was so great that Pope Clement VIII was asked to intervene. He must have been a fairly broad-minded man because before making a decision, he decided to taste the beverage for himself. He found the drink so satisfying that he gave it Papal approval and the drink has been associated with Italy ever since.

Despite such controversy, coffee houses were quickly becoming centres of social activity and communication in the major cities of Europe. In England 'penny universities' arose, so called because for the price of a penny one could purchase a cup of coffee and engage in stimulating conversation. By the middle of the 17th century, there were over 300 coffee houses in London, and individual coffee houses often attracted patrons of a similar profession or interest so that the meeting around coffee became an invaluable way of disseminating learning and experiences appropriate to those who frequented the establishments. Indeed the Jazz afternoons held at S.D. Bell's may in some way recapture this ancient purpose of the old coffee house. Jazz fans are able to share their love for this genre of music and the venue provides a platform for new musicians to express their musical abilities.

Many businesses grew out of these specialised coffee houses. Lloyd's Insurance of London owes its origins and name to Edward Lloyd who opened his coffee house around 1688 in Tower Street, London. The coffee house was frequented particularly by sailors, merchants and ship owners. Edward Lloyd ensured that they received accurate shipping news as the coffee house became known as a place which catered for those involved in shipping. It also became a place where merchants and ship

owners could arrange insurance among themselves. Eventually Lloyd's was established in its own right but retained the name of its erstwhile 'publican.'

In the mid-1600s, coffee was brought to New Amsterdam, a location later called New York by the British, further extending the global fashion for coffee consumption. As demand for the beverage continued to spread, there was intense competition to cultivate coffee outside of Arabia. Although the Arabs tried hard to maintain their monopoly, the Dutch finally succeeded in obtaining some seedlings in the latter half of the 17th century. At first they tried to cultivate a harvest from their seedlings in India but this failed. However they later found success growing them on the island of Java in what is now Indonesia. This introduced the Dutch to a growing and productive trade in coffee and soon they had expanded their coffee crops to other locations.

The Dutch did a curious thing, however. In 1714, the Mayor of Amsterdam presented a gift of a young coffee plant to King Louis XIV of France. The King ordered it to be planted in the Royal Botanical Garden in Paris. In 1723, a young naval officer, Gabriel Matthieu de Clieu obtained some seedlings from the King's plant. He set off on a journey with the objective to plant them on the island of Martinique. He endured a terrible voyage with adverse seas, weather, pirates and even a saboteur who tried to destroy the seedling. However, his journey ended with a successful planting ceremony and one seemingly indestructible seedling took root and flourished. It alone is accredited with the spread of over 18 million coffee trees on the island of Martinique. It is also the stock from which coffee trees throughout the Caribbean, South and Central America originated, including, of course, the exclusive and renowned Blue Mountain Jamaica!

Brazil also wanted in on the act and one Francisco de Mello Palheta was sent by the Emperor to French Guiana for the purpose of obtaining coffee seedlings. However, the French, not being as generous as the Dutch had once been to them, were unwilling to share. Unable to endear himself to the hard-nosed French coffee guardians, he may have purposely changed tack. The story is told that he was so fetching in appearance

Gabriel Matthieu de Clieu

to the other gender that the French Governor's wife was captivated by his presence. As a departing gift, she presented him with a large bouquet of flowers which was immediately suspicious, although it appeared not to raise any questions at the time. Buried inside the flowers he found enough coffee seeds to begin what is today a highly profitable industry.

In the space of only 100 years, coffee had established itself as a commodity crop throughout the world. As missionaries, traders and travellers of all types explored the globe on the high seas they introduced coffee seeds to lands new and old. Some plantations were successful and others came to nothing. Each one produced beans with distinct flavours according to the local soil and climate conditions and, as these plantations grew, new nations were established on coffee economies and fortunes were made and lost. By the end of the 18th century, coffee had become a chief global commodity and a goat herder called Kaldi and a few goats regretted the day they had failed to seek legal counsel and copyright protection on their discovery.

Ancient map of Brazil and vintage
botanical drawing of coffee plant

Whitmee roaster. Built 1933

COFFEE ROASTING – THE ART

*"Technological progress is like an axe in the hands
of a pathological criminal."*
Albert Einstein

In this world of progress and change there is something comforting about those few things that don't change – and roasting coffee is one of those very things – at least it certainly is at S.D. Bell's.

S.D. Bell's has been roasting coffee from all over the world for four generations. The experience of their roasters has grown over each year and individual styles, lessons and subtleties have been handed down through the generations. The quest has always been a journey of continually discovering new coffees and new subtleties of flavour.

Yet, the tried and tested roasting process has stood the test of time and remained fundamentally unchanged over the years. To get the picture, imagine an industrial, cast-iron tumble-dryer with a flame-thrower in the middle! The raw green coffee beans are introduced into the rotating drum of the roaster and the flame provides the direct heat.

Whilst every coffee producing country, and even every coffee plantation produces beans with their own individual character, most of the flavour of coffee is actually imparted through the roasting process. The individual and unique properties of the raw bean will however determine the degree to which that particular coffee should be roasted.

The process of roasting is to allow the beans to fall constantly through the flame so that over time, and in a very even manner, they slowly begin to change colour. From green, the beans first become yellow, then a light tan, until through a mid brown they turn dark brown.

The expert roaster uses the senses of sight, smell and sound and even the taste of these hot beans, to determine the precise time at which to release the roast into the cooling pan, always comparing the new roast with a 'control' roast to ensure consistency.

WELCOME TO OUR FAMILY

Barry Bell talks about a coffee roaster that is almost a member of the family in its own right.

"Although we have others, the coffee roaster used most of the time at S.D. Bell's today is a gas fired small batch roaster, our preferred method, for the following reasons:

This roaster, a "Whitmee", is a flame roaster, built in London in 1933. It has no electronics, and few points of failure. The process with most modern coffee roasters is that a rotating drum is heated externally, meaning that the drum sides are the hottest part of the apparatus. However with the internally positioned flame of the Whitmee, the hottest part of the apparatus is the flame itself which envelopes all the beans in the batch, in what can best be termed a 'democratic' manner.

Small batches (10 Kg equates to about 50,000 beans!) ensure that we only roast as much as we require at any one time. One of our greatest business imperatives is that we should never be holding more roasted coffee than we need. If that means that we have a more labour intensive process, then that is a price well worth paying to ensure that our customers receive the freshest possible product. Often this means that we roast to order."

When the beans begin to crackle it is a sign that a medium roast is ready for ejection into the cooling pan through which a fan draws air to cool the roasted beans. It is important that the beans are cooled quickly otherwise the hot beans will continue roasting and their flavour will not be as the roaster intended.

Darker roasts require even greater concentration on the part of the expert roaster. As the roast continues after the medium point is reached, the beans start to swell in the intense heat, gently releasing the natural oils that exist in every coffee bean. Depending on the moisture content of these beans, the coffee will continue to darken in the following few minutes. The smoke will turn more intense, and the crackling will increase. The coffee may be allowed to continue to cook in its own heat without a flame, depending on many factors which only the expert roaster can determine.

There are few moving parts in this process, and no electronics. In this way, the roaster adds its own personality to the roast, with a similar degree of expertise as the master cheese or wine maker applies his art.

With a final check against his control roast, the roaster releases the dark roast into the cooling pan. The sight, sound and smell of this process never fails to cause the hairs on the back of the neck to stand on end!

Developed over four generations of the Bell Family, the obsession with quality and adherence to the coffee roaster's art remains as pure and undiminished as the day it began.

COFFEE CONSUMPTION

The plethora of coffee brewing methods underlines the sheer breadth of the coffee drinking experience and tastes worldwide. First of all, a little dinner party trivia:

PERCOLATOR

This is an often misused word, which many use loosely to refer to processes such as filtering, plunging and 'espressoing', as well as percolating. In fact, the percolator describes a brewing method in which water is repeatedly boiled through a perforated chamber within a large pot. This method was invented by James Mason in 1865.

COFFEE FILTER

In 1908, Melitta Bentz, a German housewife, invented the coffee filter. She experimented with her son's school blotting paper to separate the coffee solids from the liquid, and this huge business and ubiquitous brewing method was born. The filter method produces the 'cleanest' drink as all the solids are retained separate from the liquid drink. For this reason, we recommend this method for coffees with the most subtle flavours, such as Guadeloupe Bonifieur, Kopi Luwak and Blue Mountain Jamaica.

Old S.D. Bell's advert for Melitta
aluminum coffee filter

MOKA EXPRESS

The iconic Moka Express espresso pot was invented in 1933 by Alfonso Bialetti. In the same year, Dr Ernest Illy invented the first automatic espresso machine. However, the modern-day espresso machine was created by Italian Achilles Gaggia in 1946. Gaggia invented a high pressure espresso machine by using a spring powered lever system. The first pump driven espresso machine was produced in 1960 by the Faema company.

Moka Express

KOPI LUWAK
LET THE CIVET CAT DECIDE

As with many products discovered accidentally, 'Kopi Luwak' is a bean which is retrieved through the harvesting and cleaning of droppings from the jungle floor! Plantation workers, who were banned from retaining any crop that was picked conventionally, surprised their bosses when it was discovered they were enjoying coffee that tasted far superior to the beans they were presenting at the pulping station. The game was up and one of the most sought after and expensive harvests, pound for pound, had been discovered!

"Luwak" is the Indonesian name for the civet cat, which spends its nights rampaging through the coffee plantations. They inspect each cherry meticulously and only choose to eat the ones that are perfectly ripened, containing just the right amount of water and acidity. The cat's discernment is the reason why Kopi Luwak is such highly prized coffee.

The other reason for this perfect bean is the unique processing it goes through. Once the Luwak has ingested the ripe berries, a 100% natural process begins. The intestinal enzymes and juices of the Luwak remove any bitterness leaving a perfectly 'cleansed' coffee bean. Farmed civet coffee can also be obtained which does not guarantee the ripeness of the coffee cherries, as the cat has not had the chance to choose which cherry to pick and eat.

Wild Kopi Luwak on the other hand tastes like no other. It has a full flavour, and while all other coffees exhibit changes in taste in the following seconds of the taste experience, Kopi Luwak has an unchanging, smooth, lingering aftertaste that no other coffee can equal.

Copper Turkish Ibrik with brass grinder and cups

Cowboy Pot

Neapolitian

TURKISH IBRIK

Perhaps the original coffee brewing process, this method is certainly one of the oldest. Making coffee with an Ibrik is a tricky process, involving a conical copper pot with a long handle, pulverised coffee grounds, (ideally Mocha i.e. from Ethiopia), a heat source and exact measurements of sugar and coffee. The sugar is introduced to the pot and water is added. Pulverised coffee floats on top. As the water is heated, the coffee is gradually absorbed into the liquid. It must not boil and is removed from the heat source periodically until a rich, strong soup is created. A delicious, if acquired taste.

'COWBOY POT'

The Wild West brew. Around the time when Sam Bell was hanging his own name above the former 'Dunwoody & Blakely' shop, coffee would be brewed on the range as follows: Put a good quantity of coarsely ground coffee in a tin pot. Fill the pot with fresh water from the brook. Place on the embers of the campfire, and simmer until your buddy has played 'Home on the Range.' Heat some Mexican beans, reflect on the politics of the day, and how, the gunfight at the OK Corral just six years ago has solved nothing! Pour coffee, lean back and gaze at the stars.

NEAPOLITIAN

A clever cafetière-shaped/filter-style process which allows gravity to filter boiling water through finely-ground coffee.

INSTANT

"On the Beaches". In 1901 Japanese American chemist Satori Kato of Chicago invented the first "instant" coffee. In 1906, English chemist George Constant Washington invented the first mass-produced instant coffee using dried coffee from his coffee carafe. Favoured by American GI's, instant coffee as we know it was invented in 1938, and found its calling as one of the primary motivators of the US Expeditionary Force as they progressed through Europe on the quest to defeat Hitler.

AMERICANO

Coffee drinking GI's got more than they bargained for when travelling through Italy. The 'Americano' was born through their inability to stomach a neat espresso, as served in Italy. The Italians teasingly began to refer to an espresso, adulterated with hot water, as an Americano!

CAFETIÈRE

The Cafetière or as it is often termed 'plunger' or 'French Press', creates an extremely popular 'long drink', in which the coffee grounds are allowed to infuse in hot water, before solid and liquid are separated by the plunging of a gauze disk.

'BLUE MOUNTAIN' – WHAT'S IN A NAME?

Many customers claim to enjoy 'Blue Mountain' coffee. This name is often associated with a former time and Blue Mountain coffee is often regarded as a coffee for a special occasion. In truth there are many 'Blue Mountains', as many mountain ranges reflect a blue-ish tone in the right light. Blue Mountains exist in New South Wales, and even Laurel and Hardy sang fondly of the Virginian Blue Ridge version!

In coffee terms, there are a number of Blue Mountains, notably in Kenya, and this is indeed a producing region of extremely high quality. However the classic Blue Mountain Jamaica coffee is one of the very highest quality, and while relatively cheap blends exist that contain 'BMJ'. The pure form is a drink that, like the finest Champagne should be savoured, and most advisedly brewed via a filter, rather than Cafetiere, and certainly not espresso.

The best lots of Blue Mountain are noted for their mild flavour and lack of bitterness. Over the last several decades, this coffee has developed a reputation as one of the world's most expensive and sought-after coffees. Jamaican Blue Mountain Coffee is a globally protected certification mark meaning that only coffee certified by the Coffee Industry Board of Jamaica can be labelled as such. Only coffee grown between 3,000 and 5,500 feet (1,700m) can be called Jamaica Blue Mountain. Coffee grown between 1,500 and 3,000 feet (910m) is Jamaica High Mountain, and beans grown below 1,500 feet (460m) is Jamaica Supreme or Low Mountain.

The Blue Mountains are located between Kingston to the south and Port Maria to the north. Rising to 7,500 feet (2,300m), they are some of the highest mountains in the Caribbean. The climate of the region is cool and misty with high rainfall. The soil is rich, with excellent drainage. This combination of climate and soil is ideal for coffee growing.

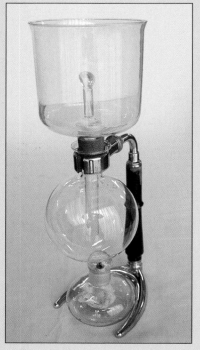
Cona

CONA

A method that is hardly used now, the Cona Company concentrates today on marketing filter machinery, despite the fact that this ingenious vacuum-driven process makes a delicious brew. Its lack of popularity can perhaps be explained by the fact that it looks somewhat intimidating, and of course, breakages are messy and expensive.

The Cona consists of a heat-resistant glass jug filled with cold water. A large glass funnel sits on top, with a pipe that reaches almost to the base of the jug, and a rubber washer holds it firmly in place. A glass stopper sits on the mouth of the funnel around which sits the medium-ground coffee.

When heat is applied, steam eventually forces the water upward into the top funnel, past the glass stopper, which prevents the coffee from falling down the pipe. Once most of the water has risen into the upper chamber, it is allowed to infuse with the coffee grounds for about three minutes.

On removal of the heat source, a vacuum is set up, drawing the liquid coffee back down, past the glass stopper, which prevents the coffee grounds from travelling with the liquid.

NATIONS CUP

Many countries, including our own, demonstrate strange contradictions when it comes to coffee consumption. For example, the Finns are connoisseurs on paper. In

Finland, more coffee is consumed per head of population than all other countries except Norway, (source Euromonitor) however many other nationalities would baulk at the standard of coffee consumed there, often filtered but left to stew until bitter.

More interesting, perhaps, is the corollary of French versus Italian taste. Espresso is popular in both France and Italy. Both nationalities' coffees will have been roasted equally darkly, and one might assume they will have similar taste profiles, but there is more to it than that. The Italian will prefer a Robusta bean, while the Frenchman chooses Arabica. Why? Well, Robusta, grown closer to sea level, grows quickly, thanks to the greater presence of oxygen, and is harvested through long periods of the year. It is an excellent cash crop, but as with many products which grow quickly, it develops less subtle flavours. Arabica, grown above 2000 feet, where there is less oxygen, benefits from slower growth. Arabica beans are more dense, and pack a fuller flavour, while producing less bitterness in the roasted product. This largely accounts for the reason why the Italian typically puts more sugar in his coffee than the Frenchman!

It is not our intention to make xenophobic comments about nationalities and their tea and coffee-drinking tastes, other than to underline the sheer breadth of tastes at play, and also to marvel at the fact that for all their variance, every nation is proud of their coffee and tea preparation expertise.

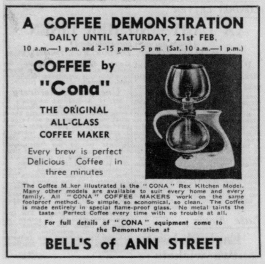

S.D. Bell's Advertising

2 DOUBLE ESPRESSO

Double espresso
2 shots (14 grams)

RISTRETTO
45ML

Ristretto
An Italian preference,
with an extremely high
concentration of coffee,
and very little liquid,
about 45ml.

+H2o
Americano

Americano – Espresso with
boiling water added. Alternatively
very long espresso, which ensures,
if correctly brewed, that a frothy
'crema' is present in the cup.
(Adding hot water to the
espresso tends to dissolve the
crema that many argue should
exist in a good espresso.)

ESPRESSO COFFEE VARIANTS

The first espresso machine was made in France in 1822. Espresso as a pure one-shot drink is commonly enjoyed throughout the world in its own right.

Fundamentally, it is a strong infusion, created by pushing boiling water through approximately seven grams of ground coffee, either by mechanical pressure or pressure created through steam, creating a drink of about 60ml. The water should not be passed too quickly through the coffee, and an automatic machine should take about twenty seconds. This also ensures that the coffee has been passed through at the correct pressure, to generate an attractive 'crema' (light brown cream) on the top.

The espresso is also used as a base for many other variants, too many to catalogue here. The variants also differ greatly by nationality, and names are often adopted from one country and applied to a different drink in another! A few of the most common variants are described in the side bars of these pages.

Several espresso variants
demand extremely hot milk,
and also frothed milk,
heated by steam.

MACCHIATO
stained

Espresso Macchiato –
the Italian 'stained' espresso.
Espresso just topped with
frothed milk.

LATTE *Milk*

Latte – Espresso, gently poured
through a generous layer
of steamed milk, with an
added layer of foam.
Latte – Macchiato – Hot milk,
'stained' with espresso.

1/3rd CAPPUCCINO

Cappuccino – Allegedly named
after Capuchin monks,
referring to the colour
of their habits.
Espresso (1/3), with a
layer of hot milk (1/3),
and topped with milk
foam (1/3). Optionally
topped with cinnamon or
chocolate powder.

TEA

THE HISTORY OF TEA

Tea is such a part of everyday life that it would be natural to regard it as a simple and mundane product, but those who regard tea as the quiet cousin of coffee could not be more mistaken. In fact, the history of tea reveals that its influence had led to greater and more significant cultural changes than coffee has ever done.

Unsurprisingly, the origins of tea lie in China. The oldest stories tell of an ancient Chinese Emperor, Shen Nung, who lived in about 2700BC.

He is credited as having invented the plough, and introduced agriculture to China and his name translated literally means 'The Divine Farmer.' However, more significantly for this book, Shen Nung is believed to have introduced tea to the Chinese people and hence is responsible for its subsequent spread throughout the world.

He was an early alchemist, developing acupuncture, herbal remedies and early Chinese medicines. It was said that his body was transparent, so that he could see what effects various natural herbs had on his body. If so, he was naturally well disposed to examine the flavours and properties of tea. However, whilst the stories of Shen Nung and Kaldi (who first noted the effect of coffee on his goats) may be somewhat mythological or at least difficult to prove, it must be said that the story of the Emperor, as told by the Chinese, is unquestionably more romantic than the one attributed to Kaldi.

The ancient myth tells of one eventful day about 4700 years ago when wild tea leaves were gently carried on the wind and landed in a bowl of water. Shen Nung tasted the resulting infusion. He was delighted by the result and remarked that it not only quenched his thirst but also lessened the desire to sleep, probably due to the caffeine within the tea. In addition, he noted that it cheered his heart.

We do not know, but it seems reasonable to assume he also recognised the flavour and tannic properties when tea leaves are left to ferment and oxidise naturally.

The Emperor-Alchemist's observations on tea still hold the approval of many who yet consider it to be a drink which is both stimulating and relaxing at the same time. It is generally accepted by many that tea 'catechins' have known anti-inflammatory, anti-oxidant, neuroprotective and anti-carcinogenic properties and that green

STORM IN A TEACUP

Most sayings have an identifiable origin. A surprising number of sayings have their origin in the Bible, such as, 'The writing is on the wall' or 'A leopard can't change its spots.' However, on this occasion the saying would appear to have originated from Cicero in the first century BC when he penned in his *De Legibus* that 'Gratidius raised a tempest in a ladle.' Ever since then people have been amending and creating their own versions so that the aforesaid storm occurs in a wash-hand basin, a cream bowl and a teacup, not to mention many other places.

The phrase which simply refers to the exaggeration of a problem making a small matter seem far greater than it really is, is also credited to Lord North who characterised the revolt of American colonists against the tax on tea as a 'tempest in a teapot'. Whilst in most parts of the world the saying is phrased as 'a storm in a tea cup', in America one is always advised not to create a 'tempest in a teapot.' We know who is right, and indeed Lord North stands justly accused of underestimating the extent and location of the storm – but we will try not to create a storm in a coffee mug by splitting hairs!

teas can reduce the risk of a number of diseases. Even today, the concentration of conference delegates in China is often revived by the inhalation of green tea, provided along with the ubiquitous bottled water (and perhaps a Mint Imperial or two!) As early as 206BC, tea was well recognised as having powerful medicinal properties and early tombs dating back to that period have been found containing tea, a measure clearly intended to protect the inhabitant in the afterlife. Tea was also pressed into 'bricks' with ruled subdivisions, to be used as units of currency. Given so many accolades, it is unsurprising that tea has developed into one of the most common drinks enjoyed in the world today.

Shen Nung's fame and his subsequent form of deification is however a little tempered by the fact that he reputedly died from toxic poisons ingested while trying out the yellow flower of a weed, which obviously offered no medicinal purpose. Retrospect, as we say, is a great thing.

TEA ADOPTION IN EUROPE

Nearer to home, the Portuguese and Dutch, being the earliest Western traders in Far Eastern textiles, silks and spices, began trading in tea in the early 17th century. Tea therefore arrived in Europe via the Dutch merchants and became very popular in the Netherlands and Portugal.

Tea reached England in the late 1650s and was made fashionable among the aristocracy when the Portuguese princess, Catherine of Braganza married Charles II in 1662, and introduced tea to the English Court.

Though coffee houses had rapidly begun to appear by this time, tea continued to be the favoured drink in the New World, so much so that the British Government used it to levy a tax to raise funds for Government, at home and abroad. The Tea Act of 1773 which received the assent of King George III opened up all kinds of problems in the American Colonies. Although the Act just levied a tax on tea, the issue epitomised the colonists' fundamental dispute that the London Members of Parliament they had not elected were able to rule their affairs in America. The dispute ended in a number of ships being returned to England with their full cargos of tea. However in Boston, a group of colonists disguised as native Americans, boarded a ship and dumped the tea cargo overboard. This later became known as 'The Boston Tea Party.'

Tea bricks showing ornate decoration and subdivisions

Some maintain that this dispute over sovereignty not only paved the way to the American War of Independence but also to a change in drinking habits of Americans who began to switch from tea to the now available alternative of coffee. It is a reminder that there is little that cannot be politicised and that even tea and coffee are not neutral when it comes to war.

Despite heavy taxation, tea still managed to become popular amongst all income groups, the poorer benefitted from an effective and extensive smuggling industry. In 1784 more tea entered Britain illegally through the Netherlands than through the official importer, the East India Company! In 1784, the British Government under William Pitt (Junior) slashed the duty levied on tea imports from a staggering 112% to only 12.5%. The aim was to assist the East India Company in reasserting its monopoly as the official tea provider in Britain. The cheaper prices resulted in the eventual universal adoption of tea drinking habits in Britain.

Postcard depicting the unloading of tea into Boston Harbour

TEA, TAO, ZEN AND THE JAPANESE TEA CEREMONY

By the fifteenth century, tea in Japan was having a very different influence. As it was noted for its enlivening, yet also calming effect, the drinking of tea became associated with cult of Taoism. When tea is drunk in such a manner and for a 'spiritual purpose' the aim is to foster harmony in humanity and nature, to discipline the mind, quiet the heart and attain a purity of enlightenment. Therefore the beverage of tea and the attached ceremony of drinking it, grew to be an excuse for the worship of purity and refinement. The ancient Japanese tea rooms evolved as a part spiritual ritual, part refreshment and part art form. Decoration sought to evoke harmony and the movements of people were perfected to happen simply and naturally. In many ways Teaism was Taoism and Zen in disguise.

In Western culture we are aware of how oriental tea packaging and small tea cups often reflect these 'spiritual' origins. Decoration is subtle, harmonious and often detailed. In the best examples there is no repetition as this would represent completion. Repetition is also seen as fatal to the imagination.

Tea was enjoyed in many English homes and high quality china tea cups and saucers were being produced from the 1700s of which the German 'Meissen,' French 'Limoges,' English 'Royal Doulton' and 'Wedgwood' varieties were the most exclusive. Until this time, Chinese tea bowls had been used, but very soon handles were introduced to the tea cup, an invention of one Robert Adams, so that ladies' delicate fingers might not be harmed!

The temperance movements of the 1850s further helped its acceptance, if any were needed, by promoting tea as an alternative to alcohol. This was quite a change from the days of 1746 when the Reverend John Wesley claimed that tea had a damaging effect on spiritual health while Dr Samuel Johnson debated with him in violent opposition. It is said that Wesley was told by a number of alcohol drinkers in London that they were heavy tea drinkers, afraid to admit to the venerable gentleman that they were drinking something much more potent. However, by 1772 Wedgwood produced a tea pot with Wesley's portrait and today Methodists drink no less tea than any other religious denomination!

In the better-off homes a 'Low Tea' was enjoyed at 4pm as a little respite between lunch and dinner although only the better off could afford to indulge. The idea of afternoon tea finds its origins in this well-heeled interval enjoyed by the upper classes and, in some minds, perhaps mistakenly, afternoon tea is still something associated with fine houses.

'High Tea' was enjoyed by the poorer and middle classes at 6pm and the terms 'low' and 'high' come from the tables at which tea was enjoyed. Low tables were used at 4pm by the ladies reclining in fine homes and gardens, whereas the poorer people sat down at a proper 'high' dinner table to enjoy their tea along with a meal.

As tea was often enjoyed by the upper classes on lawns and on picnics away from the Manor House, a little box was provided into which 'tips' were given to the waiters and staff "To Insure Prompt Service". Generally tea was consumed black, occasionally green, and milk and sugar only became popular additions from Victorian times when Chinese teas were replaced by the stronger Indian variety.

Chinese traditional teapots

FROM OPIUM TO TEABAGS

The East India Company first paid the Chinese for tea with silver as sadly there were very few Western-produced items which inspired the Chinese. Tea, heavily taxed as it entered Britain became a huge revenue earner for the Exchequer, so much so that the British Government became obsessed with its trade. "How can we continue to ensure a steady supply of such a lucrative product, when the Chinese were so protective of its export?" The answer was opium, on which thousands of Chinese had developed an insidious addiction. The British would smuggle Indian opium into China, and exchange it for tea, which, on import into Britain, would generate massive taxation revenues.

The Chinese authorities of course could not allow this, and restricted the ports into which the East India Company could trade, resulting in an expeditionary force being sent from India to force China's hand. The brutal fighting that ensued forced a militarily inept China to cede Hong Kong to the British, and allow the trade to continue.

In the 1880s, as the British saw diplomatic relations with China deteriorate, it became clear that a colonisation of India with tea plantations would secure this popular beverage for the local market – a reminder of how seemingly gentle drinks and their demand can lead to dramatic global consequences.

By 1901, India and Ceylon (Sri Lanka) tea was available in plentiful supply. It was therefore likely that when S.D. Bell started out in 1887, the bulk of his tea would have been Chinese, and Samuel is on record enjoying a pinch of Chinese 'Lapsang' in his Indian Assam brew!

To conclude our history of tea, we should perhaps end with the humble tea bag. Although now a very popular method for producing tea, it is interesting to note that tea bags were only introduced in the early 1970s. This would unquestionably have helped ladies to enjoy their afternoon tea when strolling well away from the main house – but they may not have been inclined to leave as many tips for the servants! However, we are reminded that tea and coffee are always developing and transforming and the next great change may only lie around the corner. We know only that they will both remain central to popular Western (and Eastern) culture!

Tea sample ready for tasting

"You can never get a cup of tea large enough or a book long enough to suit me."

C. S. Lewis.

THE TEA CLIPPER

Tea 'clippers' represented perhaps the most romantic age of tea exploration and commercial development. These extremely fast sailing ships were built for speed, much faster than the huge 'Merchantmen' of the East India Company. When that multi-national corporation lost its trading monopoly, it quickly became apparent that the first tea to arrive in London from any given harvest would achieve the highest price. The crew would be highly professional and well paid, and crowds would line the Thames to cheer the ships as they arrived. Competition was amazingly intense.

Famously, in the Great Tea Clipper race of 1866, four clippers, Fiery Cross, Serica, Taeping and Ariel, left Foochow on the same tide, and lost sight of each other within a day or two. Remarkably, all four arrived simultaneously into the Thames 99 days later, and the race was declared a dead heat! Clippers declined in their usefulness in 1869 with the arrival of steamships and the extra accessibility offered by the Suez Canal. The Cutty Sark, is the last surviving example of one of these wonderful pieces of 19th century marine engineering.

Montague Dawson R.S.M.A F.R.S.A
The Mighty Clippers Taeping and Ariel

With kind permission of the
MacConnal-Mason Gallery, London

TEA PROCESSING

THE TWO-MINUTE TEA EXPERT

FROM BUSH TO FACTORY

Orthodox and CTC (crush, tear and curl) are the two principal types of black teas. The two processing techniques differ considerably. In the orthodox process shoots are withered, rolled, oxidized and dried whereas in CTC process shoots are withered, rotor vane crushed, torn and curled, oxidized and dried. In the orthodox process of manufacture maceration or disruption of the leaf cell is completed in a rolling table. During rolling the juice from the leaf is extracted and the leaf is also twisted and carefully broken into smaller particles.

The objective of orthodox rolling process can be simply summarised as below:
1. To rupture the cell walls and expose their contents;

2. To bring the contents of leaf cells into contact with air to start the process of oxidation;

3. To twist the leaf and give it the desired shape or appearance;

4. To break the larger twisted pieces into smaller particles.

In the CTC process after withering and rolling, shoots are cut into tiny particles so that cell rupture is more extensive than with orthodox teas. This means that such 'tea-bag – grade' tea, whose cell structure is more exposed to the water, produces a much faster brew, often with less subtlety of flavour than teas produced by the orthodox method.

Mechanisation has developed to the extent that while all quality teas are picked by hand to ensure that only the youngest leaves are taken, over 90% of teas grown throughout the world are CTC- manufactured. They become the small, brown nutty-shaped tea types, and are graded by size, just like orthodox black-leaf teas. However the CTCs have been artificially fermented and fired in ovens rather than left to ferment naturally.

This is not to say that the tea in tea bags is fundamentally of lower quality. Indeed there are some CTC teas in tea bags that produce a fine drink. Good CTCs are widely used, and constitute well over 50% of packeted leaf teas. So it is wrong to assert that to be good tea in strength and character it must be allowed to ferment naturally and contain gold tip.

Tea arrives at the Toror tea factory, Kericho Kenya.

Old botanical drawing of tea plant Camellia Sinensis

WHAT IS TEA ?

Technically, regular tea is grown from the Camellia Sinensis var. sinensis (Chinese camellia, or larger-leafed Camellia Sinensis var. assamensis tree. It is a close relative of, and looks very like the common Camellia bush in many domestic gardens!

However the term tea has broadened to include many different herbal remedies, tisanes and infusions. S.D. Bell's, while concentrating on the traditional variety, has an increasing variety of speciality teas, which include tisanes and beverages commonly referred to as tea, but not grown from the Camellia bush.

Two leaves and a bud

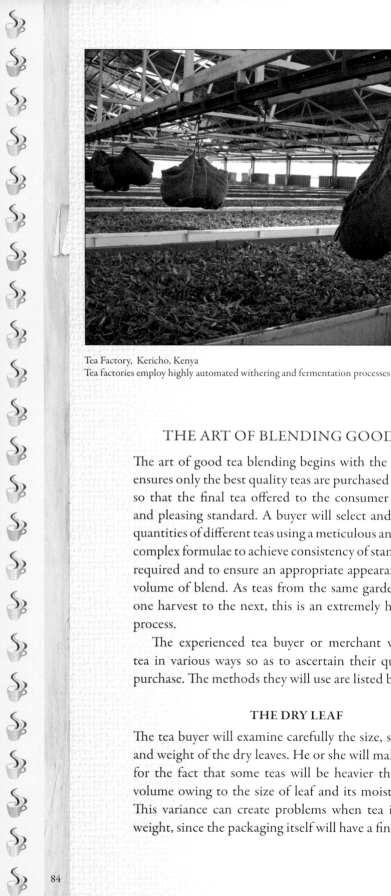

Tea Factory, Kericho, Kenya
Tea factories employ highly automated withering and fermentation processes

The CTC process ensures that the rich colour and strong aggressive flavour infuses very quickly, while teas processed in the orthodox method give a gentler, more subtle flavour and are generally a lighter colour.

Sadly much of the constituent teas in bags, in a very competitive market, is not of the best, and it could be argued that it is easier to hide an inferior product out of sight within the bag!

S.D. Bells have always specialised in the orthodox type, and will continue to do so.

THE ART OF BLENDING GOOD TEA

The art of good tea blending begins with the tasting. This ensures only the best quality teas are purchased and blended so that the final tea offered to the consumer is of a high and pleasing standard. A buyer will select and blend small quantities of different teas using a meticulous and sometimes complex formulae to achieve consistency of standard of taste required and to ensure an appropriate appearance, size and volume of blend. As teas from the same garden vary from one harvest to the next, this is an extremely highly skilled process.

The experienced tea buyer or merchant will examine tea in various ways so as to ascertain their quality before purchase. The methods they will use are listed below.

THE DRY LEAF

The tea buyer will examine carefully the size, shape, colour and weight of the dry leaves. He or she will make allowance for the fact that some teas will be heavier than others in volume owing to the size of leaf and its moisture content. This variance can create problems when tea is packed by weight, since the packaging itself will have a finite volume!

INFUSED LIQUOR

The Tea Merchant will also test the teas by immersing the leaves in boiling water.

Initially they will taste the hot tea. At this stage the tea buyer will be examining the taste and paying special attention to the resultant colour of the drink.

However, they will also allow the 'tea' to cool. As it cools he or she will observe how the appearance of the mix begins to change. This will give the expert vital information regarding the quality and nature of the tea. For example, Indian teas quickly become opaque or 'rusty' on cooling. You should be able to see this yourself if you examine a teapot of cold tea. However, poorer quality teas develop more slowly into a muddy, rather than rusty appearance on cooling. As with most things associated with teas and coffees, different tea varieties and country regions, *terroirs*, time of harvest, packing conditions and many other factors will play a part and the expert taster will apply different degrees of these tests to allow for such variances.

This also extends to the hardness of the local water, of which more anon...

The wise taster will also be keen to ensure that the tea performs well with milk, as that may well be the preferred customer taste.

Robert Bell loading tea into the tea blender

INFUSED LEAF

In this test the leaves following their infusion with hot water are "separated from liquor". Again the expert tea buyer will examine the colour, size, shape and smell of the leaf. A rich and fragrant bouquet is sought from smelling the infused leaf. The smell or "nose" of a woody character should be rejected. A copper colour is sought and a chocolate colour is rejected.

PRICE

A necessary, and somewhat prosaic factor, of course, will be the price of the tea, which of course will vary year on year, depending on seasonal factors, supply and demand, currency fluctuations and the fact that tea, along with many other agricultural 'softs' has become a very highly traded global commodity, just like copper, tin, oil, gold or pork bellies. While the blender's greatest concern is to achieve the best possible tea at the best possible price, commercial imperatives also demand that his customers are protected from dramatic increases in price!

TYPICAL ORTHODOX LEAF GRADINGS

Special Finest Tippy Golden Flowery Orange Pekoe

Flowery Broken Orange Pekoe

Golden Broken Orange Pekoe

Curled Torn Crushed

P	Pekoe	A wiry, large broken leaf usually without golden tips. Sri Lanka produces large amounts of Pekoe.
OP	Orange Pekoe	Refers to a high quality thin, wiry leaf rolled more tightly and picked later in the year than F.O.P.
FOP	Flowery Orange Pekoe	Refers to high quality whole leaf tea made from the first two leaves and bud of the shoot. India produces large amounts of this grade.
GFOP	Golden Flowery Orange Pekoe	The golden refers to the colourful tips at the end of the top bud.
TGFOP	Tippy Golden Flowery Orange Pekoe	GFOP, but with larger amount of tips.
SFTGFOP	Special Finest Tippy Golden Flowery Orange Pekoe	The highest quality with more tips than TGFOP.
S	Souchong	A twisted leaf picked from the bottom of the tea bush. China produces this grade used in their pinewood smoked teas, such as Lapsang.
BROKEN LEAF TEAS PRODUCE A DARKER CUP AND INFUSE FASTER THAN WHOLE LEAF TEAS.		
BOP	Broken Orange Pekoe.	A small, flat broken leaf with medium body.
FBOP	Flowery Broken Orange Pekoe	Increasingly larger, 'tippier' teas.
GBOP	Golden Broken Orange Pekoe	Increasingly larger, 'tippier' teas.
GFBOP	Golden Flowery Broken Orange Pekoe	Increasingly larger, 'tippier' teas.
OTHER		
F	Fannings	Crushed leaf which infuses very quickly, a very strong brew. Also used in teabags and vending machines.
PF	Pekoe Fannings	Crushed leaf which infuses very quickly found in superior teabags.
PD	Pekoe Dust	Small grade, used in mass marketed tea bags and vending machines.
CTC	Curled Torn Crushed	Larger grade for tea bags and strong loose tea.

S.D. Bell's Tea Bags - Pekoe Fannings

PREPARATION OF THE PERFECT CUP OF TEA

The Japanese Ceremony would demand that we take two hours, sitting cross-legged on a hard bench or futon. Well, here are a few other, simpler principles, which take into account our busy lifestyles and which might help your general enjoyment of a fine cup of tea.

WHAT YOU WILL NEED

Use quality tea - preferably 'orthodox' leaf tea, for a more subtle and interesting flavour. As a general rule, the larger the leaf, the more satisfying the drink.

If tea bags must be used, then brew in a pot, rather than a simple bag in the mug process, due to the 'milk in first' principle, discussed below.

Contrary to received wisdom this does not need to be a silver tea pot - a glass, china or stainless steel pot that keeps the infusion hot are all equally fit for purpose. Clay, pottery and delft pots do not keep the brew sufficiently warm. Serve your fine brew in a cup that retains its heat but, again, this need not necessarily be a china cup! If the environment and atmosphere are important to you, a china cup and saucer will add to the occasion. But then so will a cucumber sandwich and a chamber orchestra and the presence of fine company!

WHAT YOU WILL NEED TO DO

Warm the pot, introduce the leaves, adding a teaspoonful for the pot if desired. Use freshly boiled water, as tea brews best in water with high oxygen content. Give the tea time to brew. This can be anything from one minute to six or seven, depending on the tea: the finer the grade, the faster the infusion. Stir the pot and let the leaves settle. Many beautiful teas are enjoyed as an unbroken leaf which releases its flavour over an hour or more and so produces consecutive cups over an entire evening in front of the television! With quality teas, it is perfectly acceptable to add a second dose of boiling water.

It would be easy to forget that the major ingredient in tea and coffee is actually water. The hardness of the water can have a huge impact, as hard water takes longer to draw the flavour out of the leaf. For many years, S.D. Bell's sold 'Hard Water Tea' in large quantities. This tea blend contained a high proportion of Ceylon tea, (from Sri Lanka), which is naturally rich and 'malty'.

> *Would you drink a fine Champagne out of a polystyrene cup?*
>
> *Only if there was no alternative!*

HOW WILL YOU HAVE YOUR WATER TODAY SIR?

Water hardness is caused by dissolved calcium and, to a lesser extent magnesium, which occurs naturally in the water. We generally associate this with the rather ugly deposition of scale which occurs in kettles, irons and dishwashers. As a rule water is harder around the central region of Northern Ireland and soft on the East and West areas of Northern Ireland. However, apart from a small region around the West Fermanagh, and Dungannon and Armagh areas which are classified as hard water, the majority of N.Ireland is on the soft side rather than hard. The expert tea and coffee producer knows the effect water hardness can have on tea and coffee and will compensate accordingly by the way of their blends.

The owners of large and fine houses with their own water sources were often concerned that the tea they served should make allowance for their particular water. Generations of Bells have blended bespoke teas specifically for individuals according to their taste and the water types of their homes.

On one occasion an unnamed Earl entered the premises of S.D. Bell's with a water sample taken from the pure spring water that flowed naturally at his residence. Barry took the water sample, opened it and immediately remarked to the Earl that this water was indeed unique among all other waters, as it had a very distinct whisky flavour. Barry, tactful as ever, suggested to the Earl that he return with another water sample, but must ensure that the whisky bottle is rinsed next time!

THE BIG QUESTION – ARE YOU PRE- OR POST-LACTIC?

Are you pre or post-lactic? This is a question which can destroy a good dinner party. Should the milk go in first, or follow as an addition to the hot beverage? Well, allow this book to bring you the definitive answer. Milk should be placed in the cup first and the hot tea added to it.

Now for the science bit. Milk is a *colloid*, a liquid whose elements are not chemically connected and can easily be separated. This separation happens easily when it is poured into hot tea.

Milk, of course, is a matter of taste, and its use varies depending on the type of tea and the drinker. With black teas, skimmed, half-fat, full fat and cream are all acceptable. Cream was the preference of the Victorians, and when travelling in India today, you may often still be offered cream as a result. Northern Germans feel the same, while directors at S.D. Bell's divide themselves between black and semi-skimmed. All these are quite acceptable and remind us that even after the expert tea blender has done his job we continue to contribute to the craft of personalising our own tea, according to our tastes and whims.

Obviously where circumstances demand a bag in a cup, most people will introduce the milk later, but at the risk of offending some, such drinkers will hardly care whether the milk has been degraded in the process or not! It has to be said, however, that a cup of tea, brewed in even the most primitive surroundings, has the power to revive. By the roadside in Malaysia you will be encouraged to enjoy warm tea in a plastic bag through a drinking straw. On top of a frosty Slieve Donard you may regard the post-lactic brew in a Thermos as the finest and most welcome cuppa ever consumed by a human being!

PRE-LACTIC POST-LACTIC

THE MIRACLE OF TEA INTO WINE

Many still lament the passing of the iconic tea chest. However the present cartons, and paper/foil sacks are much lighter, easier and cheaper to transport, and do not leak nails, woodchips and other foreign bodies into the loose tea. In particular, chests were found to be ideal containers when moving house. At S.D. Bell's we often still receive requests for them, whether for house moves, for theatrical productions or for the rhythm section of musical 'skiffle groups'!

Paul, an S.D. Bell's regular, describes another use, which may have given our founder cause for concern, were he in a position to hear of this potentially nefarious use:

"My experience of seeing a Bell's tea chest being used for something other than transporting tea was down to my father-in-law. Many years ago, he was a keen home wine maker. One of the problems he faced was keeping the fermenting wine at a constant temperature. He solved the problem by placing four glass wine demijohns into a Bell's tea chest, which was silver foil lined and by placing a 10 –15 watt light bulb into the chest for a heat source. Once a lid was placed over the chest the contents achieved a constant temperature night and day at a very low running cost. The wine fermented more quickly using this method and was therefore ready for drinking much sooner. Needless-to-say the wine never lasted very long so the Bell's tea chest was always in use."

An old S.D. Bell's tea chest, now highly collectable

"OH, THANK YOU SARGE!"

"Tea cleared my head and left me with no misapprehensions"
—DUKE OF WELLINGTON

Old tea postcards

Coffee and tea culture is not a 1990s phenomenon as evidenced by the vintage postcards pictured and the following piece of music written by Bach. In the latter 18th century piece, the performers debate whether coffee is a healthy habit, a discussion which continues today!

BACH'S COFFEE CANTATA BWV 211
GERMAN LIBRETTO BY CHRISTIAN FRIEDRICH HENRICI, TRANSLATED BY ROBERT BELL

Composed for performance by Bach's Collegium at Zimmerman's Coffee House, Leipzig, between 1732 and 1734.

Recitative Narrator
Be quiet, stop your chatter, and pay attention to what's happening: here comes Herr Schlendrian [literally "Stuck in the Mud!]with his daughter Lieschen; he's growling like a bear. Hear for yourselves, what she has done to him!

Aria - Schlendrian
Don't our children cause us endless trials & tribulations! Everything I say to my daughter Lieschen every day seems fruitless.

Recitative - Schlendrian
You wicked child, you disobedient girl, when will I ever get my way; give up coffee!

Lieschen
Father, don't be so severe! If I can't drink my bowl of coffee three times a day, then in my suffering I will be like a shrivelled up piece of roast goat meat.

Aria - Lieschen
Mmmmm! how sweet the coffee tastes, more delicious than a thousand kisses, mellower than muscatel wine. Coffee, coffee I must have, and if someone would like to give me a treat, mmmm, then pour me a cup of coffee!

Recitative - Schlendrian
If you don't give up coffee drinking then you won't go to any wedding feast, nor out promenading. Oh! When will I get my way; give up coffee!

Lieschen
Oh well! Just leave my coffee there!

Schlendrian
Now I've got the little monkey! I won't get you that
fashionable whalebone skirt.

Lieschen
I can easily live with that.

Schlendrian
You're not to stand at the window and watch people
as they pass by!

Lieschen
That's fine, only I beg of you, leave me my coffee!

Schlendrian
And I won't be giving you any silver or gold ribbons
for your bonnet!

Lieschen
Yes, yes! Just let me enjoy myself!

Schlendrian
You disobedient Lieschen you, so you agree with all
my demands!

Aria - Schlendrian
Stubborn girls are not so easily won over. Yet when we
find their weak spot, ah! then we have success.

Recitative - Schlendrian
Now heed what your father says!

Lieschen
In everything but the coffee.

Schlendrian
Right, you'll have to resign yourself to never taking a
husband.

BARRY'S BREW

Barry Bell chats about his favourite teas, and discusses
how tea tastes have changed:

"Tea drinkers' tastes have become very varied through the last four decades, but our backbone remains our House Blend: Natural Leaf Tea. The Natural Leaf blend originates from India (Assam), with additional Ceylon (from Sri Lanka). Ceylon teas are noted for their malty, full flavour.

A firm favourite of mine is an orthodox leaf from the Kenyan Milima plantation. It has a large 'tippy' leaf and delightful flavour. Almost all Kenyan teas are manufactured as CTCs for the tea bag and vending industries. Many of these are good teas, and S.D. Bell's also produces tea bags which contain pure Kenyan CTC.

Many teas: black, semi-fired, green and white come from China, some of which are infused with flower petals and perfumes, and we stock many such teas. Most popular, however, remain Green "Gunpowder" and smoked "Lapsang Souchong" teas.

Darjeeling is recognized as perhaps the 'Champagne' of teas. It is protected by a 'PDO' mark, similar to those which champagne and parmesan cheese enjoy. Exclusively from West Bengal, India it must be grown from the small-leafed Chinese camellia, and particularly in the early harvests ("first flush") does not fully turn dark brown like its Indian cousin, but stays greenish in colour, and produces a delightfully fresh, aromatic and fruity drink.

Herbal teas are gaining in popularity. We sell a lot of South African Rooibos picked from the indigenous 'Red Bush'. The drink is refreshing, very mild and caffeine-free. Green teas with added ginger, and black teas with cinnamon, cloves, lemon peel and nutmeg are also particularly popular, and although not to my taste, illustrate that the availability of so many varieties and the demand for customer choice continue to drive the business.

It pleases us greatly that our best teas come from India and Ceylon, where in a great many gardens the turbine machinery that still dries the leaves and aids their fermentation, originates from the Sirocco Works of Belfast."

Lieschen
Oh yes! Father, a husband!

Schlendrian
I swear it won't happen.

Lieschen
Unless I can forgo coffee? ...From now on, coffee, remain left alone! Father, listen, I won't touch a drop!

Schlendrian
Then you shall have a husband at last!

Aria - Lieschen
Today my dear father, do it right now! Oh, a husband! Really, that suits me wonderfully! If only it should come about before I go to bed, that instead of a cup of coffee I were to get a fine lover!

Recitative - Narrator
Old Schlendrian goes away at once to seek a husband for his daughter Lieschen; however Lieschen secretly lets it be known: no bachelor may come to my house unless he promises me, and it is also written into our contract of marriage, that I may make coffee for myself whenever I want!

Trio
A cat can't stop catching mice, and maidens remain faithful to their coffee. Mothers love their coffee, grandmothers drink it too. Who are we to deny the daughters?

LADY LONDONDERRY'S TEA AND MOUNT STEWART HOUSE

Occasionally, the management at S.D. Bell's is asked to come up with new and personalised blends, some of which can become very popular in their own right. One such was Lady Londonderry's Tea, when the firm was approached by the National Trust at Mount Stewart House, near Greyabbey, on the Ards Peninsula, County Down.

This grand estate was acquired by the Stewart family in 1744, using the proceeds of the sale of their interest in the East India Company. To come up with a tea which the Lady of the House might have blended herself, and kept in a locked caddy (as was the norm for such a valuable household commodity), was the challenge. Furthermore, it should be a tea that might suit 21st century tastes.

Robert and Barry took to researching the history of the House, and those who were associated with it. Of course at the time the house was built, all tea came from China. A regular visitor at Mount Stewart was one Thomas Lipton, who was perhaps the greatest landowner in Ceylon, now Sri Lanka. (Lipton had spotted his chance when Ceylon's huge coffee crop

Robert Bell presents a box of Lady Londonderry's Tea to HRH Prince Charles at Mount Stewart House

Newtownards Chronicle
20 May 2010

Following the garden tour, the prince viewed many of the portraits, sculptures and pieces of memorabilia, including the famous Hambletonian 'Rubbing Down' painting by 18th century artist, George Stubbs.

He then met guests at a reception in the central hall, including Trust volunteers, staff and suppliers.

Robert Bell, whose great grandfather established S. D. Bell & Co, purveyors of fine tea and coffee, explained to the prince the provenance of the Lady Londonderry's tea.

"In the time of Edith, Lady Londonderry, it would have been customary for the lady of the house to blend her own tea," he related.

"I explained it was a Chinese afternoon tea, with a little Ceylon, because of the association of Thomas Lipton with Mount Stewart.

"He took a packet of the tea and said he was looking forward to enjoying it in the afternoon," Mr Bell continued. "I am honoured that he should take it. I found him charming and very interested."

Lady Londonderry's Tea

selected and blended by S D Bell & Co, Ltd., Belfast

was blighted, rendering the region unproductive for coffee. He bought up large tracts of land and created very productive tea plantations.) So it is probable that Lipton will on occasion have introduced strong, malty Ceylon to Mount Stewart. In keeping with modern tastes, some high grown Assam just had to make it into the blend. Thus, Lady Londonderry's Tea was born and it continues to sell in Mount Stewart house and at S.D. Bell's!

Robert was honoured to present a box to HRH Prince Charles, Prince of Wales, President of the National Trust, in May 2010.

RAISED ON BELL'S TEA

Lisnakea's irrepressible Mr Pat Cassidy swore by Bell's tea and its usefulness to sustain all creatures, even vegetables. His champion 'super-sized potatoes' were fed on Bell's tea and grew to over 8 foot 4 inches tall. He told his local newspaper how he wrote to S.D. Bell's explaining the tipple his plants enjoyed. They immediately responded and sent 2 lb of their tea to assist in his mammoth agricultural efforts.

From that day Pat became an ardent fan of Bell's tea and his neighbours used to benefit from a refreshing cup of the same at his harvest soirees.

FINAL WORDS

Compiling this book has been a labour of love. Memories have wafted back and forth like the aroma of a coffee roast in Ann Street, blended with new seasons' teas and seasoned with all the spices of Araby! In a sense that reads like just a list of ingredients, but the mix of experiences which this book records is one which only human spirit and time can create.

The writing of this book has stirred in me recollections of so many people; loyal, hard-working staff, sadly too numerous to name and many with twenty or thirty years' of service to their credit. Such people were, and still are, the backbone of S.D. Bell's. Today we move forward, with a young and energetic workforce and no firm could ask for more.

In the past the Bells and their staff have pulled more than just their own weight but this would have been of no significance were it not for our customers – a wonderful cross section of people we feel privileged to call our friends.

Friends they became, in the truest sense of the word, because in austere times we became aware of their families, their needs and the challenges they faced. In times of rationing people learned to value the little things, like a tin of fruit or a chocolate biscuit in a way they may not have done before. Only a company with a long history can claim to have been through such days with their customers, developing relationships and trust which would be the envy of any business.

Our customers have become friends whether they come to us through the coffee house, the emporium, the online shop or as other retail and wholesale businesses. Over the years we have also developed firm friendships with suppliers at home and

abroad, without whom life would have been harder and less fulfilling. Whatever the association, it is our unswerving goal, to develop the same depth of relationships today and so to find new friends that will last for future generations.

To you, our readers, may I thank you for showing an interest in our firm. I hope that you have enjoyed the stories and have been informed in the art of coffee and tea. Now we draw our book to a gentle close, confident that we will continue to offer our customers the very best of these two fine beverages.

W.B.S. Bell

W.B.S. Bell

Published by Woodstone Books

Woodstone Studios
48 Church Road
Crossgar
County Down
Northern Ireland
BT30 9HR

www.woodstonebooks.com

Historical consultant: Aidan Campbell
Consultant editor: Deborah Drury

Printed in Slovenia
First published 2012

ISBN 978-0-9574040-0-7